# THE
# POLITICS
# OF
# URBAN
# PLANNING
# POLICY

16

$\xi\xi Q$

# Books of the Jerusalem Center for Public Affairs Related to Local Government

*Local Government, Democracy and Elections in Judea and Samaria: Legal Aspects*, by Moshe Drori (Hebrew, 1980)

*Project Renewal: Urban Revitalization Through Partnership*, by Paul King, Orli HaCohen, Hillel Frisch and Daniel J. Elazar (1987)

*Local Government in Israel*, edited by Daniel J. Elazar and Chaim Kalchheim (Hebrew, 1987; English, 1988)

*Religious Institutions in the Political System: The Religious Councils in Israel*, by Eliezer Don-Yehiya (Hebrew, 1988)

*The Politics of Urban Planning Policy*, by Efraim Torgovnik (1990)

*Urban Revitalization: Israel's Project Renewal and Other Experiences*, edited by Daniel J. Elazar (1990)

# THE
# POLITICS
# OF
# URBAN
# PLANNING
# POLICY

## Efraim Torgovnik

UNIVERSITY
PRESS OF
AMERICA

Lanham
New York
London

THE JERUSALEM
CENTER FOR PUBLIC
AFFAIRS

# University Press of America®, Inc.

4720 Boston Way
Lanham, Maryland 20706

3 Henrietta Street
London WC2E 8LU England

Co-published by arrangement with
The Jerusalem Center for Public Affairs

Managing Editor: Mark Ami-El
Typesetting: Custom Graphics and Publishing, Ltd., Jerusalem

## Library of Congress Cataloging-in-Publication Data

Torgovnik, Efraim.
The politics of urban planning policy / Efraim Torgovnik.
p.   cm.
1.  City planning—Israel.   2.  Urban policy—Israel.
I. Title.
HT169.I8T67   1990   307.1'216'091724—dc20   90–33556 CIP

ISBN 0-8191-7795-4 (alk. paper)
ISBN 0-8191-7796-2 (pbk. : alk. paper)

*To My Wife*

*Virginia*

# ACKNOWLEDGMENTS

Financial aid for this study was generously provided by the Research Committee of the Faculty of Social Sciences, Tel Aviv University. Special thanks are due to Tony Graham for his editorial assistance, and to Mark Ami-El, whose aid in preparing the book for typesetting was invaluable. My thanks to Sylvia Weinberg, who was helpful in typing the manuscript. I am grateful to my colleagues for their helpful comments: Elisha Efrat of the Geography Department, Tel Aviv University, who read Chapter 2; Rachel Alterman of the Planning and Architecture Department, the Technion; and Mrs. Tsophia Santo, who read Chapter 3. Sole responsibility for the manuscript lies with the author.

# CONTENTS

# LIST OF TABLES AND MAPS

# GLOSSARY

AL – Association of Landowners

CPAL – Committee for the Preservation of Agricultural Land

LPBC – Local Planning and Building Commission

RPBC – Regional Planning and Building Commission

NPBC – National Planning and Building Council

LMA – Land Management Authority

Labor Alignment – Coalition of Labor Parties and Factions

Likud – Center-Right Party

Mapam – Leftist Labor Party

Rafi – A Labor Faction with the Labor Alignment

*Haaretz* – Major Daily Newspaper

*Maariv* – Evening Newspaper

*Yediot Achoronot* – Evening Newspaper

# FOREWORD

## Daniel J. Elazar

Israel is a country of many paradoxes. As a social democratic state with a strong socialist background that emerged after a period of colonial administration, it was born with a strong central government and with every inclination on the part of its leaders to further centralize power. In fact, however, within a formally highly centralized framework, power is highly diffused in practice, with every person or institution able to secure some measure of power, holding on to it in ways that approach absurdity.

In fact, it often seems that Israelis have a deep-seated aversion to planning or at least to carrying out plans in matters governmental. In practice, it means the slow making of many plans and the rapid violation of them once adopted. The study of urban planning policy in Israel, then, is a daunting task.

Efraim Torgovnik, one of the senior professors of government, state-local relations, and urban affairs in Israel, himself an elected member of the Tel Aviv City Council, has tackled this daunting subject, drawing upon his many years of study and involvement in the planning process, combining academic detachment with personal experience. In this book he examines Israel's urban planning policy from all its aspects, but he properly emphasizes the politics of urban planning policy. He is concerned with state, local, and private roles within the process.

Professor Torgovnik approaches the subject with full understanding of the secondary importance of urban settlement in the original Zionist enterprise, which was a classic late nineteenth century, intellectual, "back-to-the-land" movement, and how the state born of that enterprise had to come to grips with the fact that, despite the great success of the kibbutzim and moshavim, reality dictated that 90 percent of its population would be living in urban areas, ideology notwithstanding. He considers the other great Zionist issue of population dispersal, an effort to establish roots in as much of the Land of Israel as possible so as to consolidate Jewish claims in face of the Israel-Arab dispute and the security considerations that flowed from it. Finally, he considers the problem of urban rehabilitation in the wake of pressured settlement of masses of new immigrants in the early days of the state.

xv

Professor Torgovnik considers both the structural and normative determinants of planning policy. He examines the problems of state-local relations and urban growth. He relates all this to the unique Israeli situation where 93 percent of all land in the state is owned or controlled by the state lands authority.

Professor Torgovnik wisely understands that the politics of urban planning policy in Israel must be seen in the larger context of the Zionist enterprise which has willy-nilly set the boundaries within which urban development and redevelopment continue to take place. Here we have another set of paradoxes. Zionism, in its effort to revolutionize the Jewish condition, sought to base the settlement of Eretz Israel on a massive return to the land. Yet most of the Jews sought the cities. More than that, they sought to live in the most densely populated parts of the country, in the center of things, as it were.

This ancient Jewish trait of wanting to be at the center of the action goes back to the very earliest days of the Jewish people 4,000 years ago. As far as we can see, Abraham himself was a semi-nomadic trader who settled in the heart of the fertile crescent, on the trade routes between Egypt and Mesopotamia. Ever since then, the descendents of Abraham have sought the center of the dominant communications networks of every age, which is why they have been so prominent in human affairs, so visible in world history, and so vulnerable to their enemies. In that respect, the original Zionist idea was truly counter-cultural, although Eretz Israel itself is located at the crossroads of the Eurasian and African land masses, astride a continental divide between the Mediterranean-Atlantic watershed on one side and the Indian Ocean-Pacific watershed on the other.

No back-to-the-land movement or even efforts at population dispersal seriously alter such a deeply embedded cultural trait. Hence, the directions which the state wished to impose on urban planning policy were being challenged by the realities of the Jewish people all the time, even where there was ideological agreement among the political leaders and planners as to what needed to be done.

Planners in the local authorities had to take the reality as it came. It did little good for a planner sitting in Petah Tikva or Holon to try to reflect the dictates of Zionist ideology while thousands of people were coming to settle within their municipal boundaries and dozens of contractors were grabbing land to build them apartments and thereby profit from the process.

Thus another tension was introduced. In principle, the planning process was to be technical, but Israel is a state where ideological movements and political parties are very strong and most things are, in the course of affairs, politicized. This was even more true during the first generation of statehood than today. Urban planning could not escape politics, either on the macro level or the micro. To this, add the normal interorganizational politics of competing ministries, authorities, and political personalities, the normal public-private conflicts, the special problem of private interests in Israel, and the complexity grows.

In sum, just as the highly complex politics of Israel rests on a series of paradoxes and often competing fundamental expectations or demands, so, too, does the planning process in Israel as a matter of course. These great paradoxes and tensions seem to be built into Israel's civil society. It is the task of both politics and planning to come to grips with them, to prevent them from being so dysfunctional that nothing can be achieved, but to recognize that they are part of the warp and woof of the Israeli polity and cannot be dismissed or ignored.

In this book Professor Torgovnik lays out these paradoxes, tensions, dysfunctionalities, and conflicts in the realm of urban planning policy and analyzes them for us with clarity, vigor, and comprehensiveness. As such, this book represents another contribution to the small but growing literature on local government, state-local relations, and urban affairs in Israel. The Jerusalem Center for Public Affairs prides itself on being one of the principal institutions concerned with these issues. It is very pleased to be able to add this volume to its previous studies of local government in Israel, Israel's local religious councils, local government and law in Judea and Samaria, and its studies of the municipal elections in Israel.

# PREFACE

The politics of urban planning policy in Israel is discussed here in term of two related issues, both of which are rooted in Israel's short history. The first concerns the systemic structural and normative features of state domination, intervention and control, which accompanied the process of nation building and development. This resulted in a highly centralized policy-making system within a welfare state framework. The planning policy structures that emerged delineated state and local roles, urban decision structures, and organizations and agencies with access to decision-making policy; these structures also introduced an exclusionary principle to others. The second issue concerns the growth of the urban sector, which was due to market forces and which took place against a background of preferential systemic social investments in the rural sector.

The conflicts that emerged under the conditions outlined above relate to pressures for greater access to policy arenas for local units, individuals and groups. Within the delimiting systemic features of state control, the politics of planning policy emerged in a setting of a parallel and multi-actor decision structure. Conflict is not related to class interests nor to public participation in the urban sector. Rather, an organizational diversity underlies the planning policy decisions system, which reflects the basic political structure of the state and the local setting. Within this structure the state has a key role but is exposed to conflict, which is bred by the aforementioned diversity. The conflict of individuals in state and local planning agencies — and the conflict between them and the agencies and organizations involved in urban planning policy — is the central theme of this work.

The approach adopted is to relate urban empirical findings to theoretical political questions. Planning policy, like any policy area, is related to politics. The politics of planning policy is analyzed on the basis of observation of the making of planning policy in Jerusalem and Tel Aviv — two of the three major urban centers in Israel — and by relating systemic elements to political issues of power and influence, and the relations and links between the state and the local setting. Thus, much of the analysis focuses on the conflict for dominance over planning policy and conflict resolution.

Chapter 1 outlines the major theoretical positions, namely that political analysis is the major explanatory basis for urban planning policy. Chapter 2 analyzes the systemic support for the rural sector, the emergence of the urban setting by market forces, and the polarized structure that emerged. Chapters 3 and 4 relate two sides of the same coin. The diverse structure of strategy control, and the conflicts generated thereby, is analyzed in chapter 3; the structural expression of systemic features of state control and the conflict base (and regulation) it provides in urban land-use and development policy is discussed in chapter 4. Chapters 5 and 6 deal with planning policy conflict and implementation in Jerusalem and Tel Aviv, respectively. Analysis underscores the the parallel and often dominant role of the state vis-à-vis local government in planning policy in Jerusalem and the role of ideology (chapter 5); and the dynamics of evolved local efforts for dominance vis-à-vis the state's urban ideology (chapter 6).

The political analysis of planning policy in Israel points to changes, due to the prevalence of the politics of planning policy, in state and local roles. We have tried here to indicate some of the ramifications of these changes. What is sure is that whatever the degree of balance between state and local in urban planning policy and implementation, the degree of conflict will remain as severe as it has been ever since the First Aliyah.

# Chapter 1

# THE POLITICAL AND ORGANIZATIONAL FRAMEWORK OF PLANNING

This book is about the politics of planning policy. The various structural and normative features that determine the conflictual nature of such politics are discussed in the broad context of the inter-organizational setting of central-local relationships. The highly politicized Israeli setting is used here as a basis for generalizations which are considered to be relevant to other, similar systems.

In attempting to discover the politics and systemics of planning policy in Israel, discussion will focus on the channels of influence available to those who are active in central and local planning organizations. We shall try to determine whether changes in substantive planning policy come about as a result of conflict resolution, and whether such resolutions follow the dominant political lead of the time. We shall look into the political and institutional constraints on planning policy, and the translation mechanisms (and networks) that relate normative positions or ideologies to planning policy decisions. The theoretical issues to be addressed are: (1) political concepts useful in analyzing planning policy conflicts, and (2) the conditions that activate planning policy issues.

Underlying the analysis is the Israeli local-state,[1] which translates its intensive role in the economy, urban and regional domains and other spheres of life, to a political institutional arrangement (including mediating organizations) where structure is related to action. In a planning policy domain (indeed, in any policy domain) the state is not expected to remain a passive or minor actor. The nature of its role and relative power in the planning policy domain is determined here empirically. Data and analysis presented here deal with political behavior and process of individuals, interests and organizations, and not structure per se. Policy, conflict and central-local interactions and interrelations are converged here with empirical data.

The state's involvement in the politics of urban planning policy decisions is viewed here as the central government's effort to

1

control and predict its political environment. The state role allows us to delineate normative policy outcomes. The role of central authorities creates uncertainty for the local unit; hence it is essential to analyze the links and interactions between regional and national organizations. The contact that regional and national officials have with the local urban level includes intervention in the planning policy domain. In terms of two recent theoretical approaches to urban studies — the neo-Weberian and neo-Marxist approaches[2] — we shall show policy interactions with interventive aims by regional and national officials and organizations in the local level of planning policy activity. In addition to the structural elements pursued in this book, the analysis follows the managerial direction. We thus deal with individuals and organizations, and their decision-making processes, involved in the politics of planning policy.

Intervention takes place in a structured context where action and relative power can be exercised in a variety of networks, with systemic constraints on all actors be they local, regional, or national. In discussing the larger concept of society's social structure Lukas stated: "Social life can only properly be understood as a dialectic of power and structure, a web of possibilities for agents whose nature is both active and structured, to make choices and pursue strategies...."[3] The importance of the relationship of structure and power is also underscored in Saunders' study of urban politics and policy.[4] We relate structure and power to the concept of access to planning policy decisions. Access can be formal — based on systemic arrangements; or it can emerge as part of a political policy conflict — by interests which react to a public policy issue. In both instances the type and utilization of access must be identified. Additionally, we will look at whether inaction, for example, is a result of a decision by those who have formal access and occupy positions of decision-power and will seek to identify systemic structural features which either share access or exclude actors, organizations or interests from the planning policy decision arena.

## The Planning Process: Procedural or Political?

Political analysis of planning policy is now recognized as a missing dimension in planning theory. Take, for example, the following two recent statements: "Planning theory is not produced in a social vacuum. It is produced by individuals in concrete social situations who are trying to explain, justify, or change planning in their particular context."[5] "The view that planning is, above all else, a political activity...has only recently and grudgingly been accepted...this was because the professional ideology was essentially one that claims that planning was objective, technical, and as such not political."[6] Notwithstanding these comments, there is no theory of planning which is anchored solidly in either politics or policy.

A political-policy focus of planning moves beyond the questions of how things are done professionally and technically (as Faludi has done in his important procedural planning theory), to the making and the products of planning policy and the change it generates on the environment. Secondly, the political policy focus recognizes an underlying view of the mode of achieving rationality in planning. Goals are set and implemented by resolving conflict among a variety of actors; consensus is achieved through mutual accommodations and continuous interaction. In actual planning decisions this is essential because of systemic structural and normative features which determine access to planning decisions. In short, planning organizations — institutionalized and ad hoc (pressure groups) — are a reflection of the political forces in society. Analysis of planning decision situations indicates a pluralistic policy setting. Research, therefore, should be directed to the participants in planning (technicians, politicians, bureaucrats, councilmen, mayors, etc.), the conflicts involved, and the use of politics to resolve conflict and rationalize planning. Such emphasis denies not only the technical nature of planning but also a possible bureaucratic model, which would assume that professional planning decision makers within a given hierarchy are able to identify the public interest and act on its behalf. Thus the political focus translates itself into an investigation of the actions in planning policy decisions. We can therefore speak of systemic determinants of planning policy (which also identify those who are excluded from planning policy decisions), the conditions which give access to decision, and the outcomes. The approach used here does not deny the importance of procedural aspects of planning. In dealing with systemic structural and normative determinants of planning as well as the politics of planning policy, we assert that they are the basis for the explication of both procedural and substantive elements.

Lastly, in the political view of planning policy we make a distinction between planning organizations that are systemically

3

assigned to make planning decisions, and organizations that become involved and seek access to planning decisions (in order to exacerbate conflict, introduce new demands, etc.). To sum up, we argue that procedural and substantive elements of planning as well as planning policy products are understood in terms of the politics of planning policy.

Procedural Planning Theory (PPT) deals with means and with the "making and implementing of plans."[7] The PPT not only overlooks important environmental determinants of planning decisions but disregards the political (conflict) basis of planning decisions. The PPT is not a proper guide to planning as a human activity which involves conflicting goals. As noted by Thomas: "Politics has been removed from its control position in society and replaced by the methodology of planning."[8] The need to supplement the PPT has been noted in a recent symposium on planning theory, where various theoretical positions were identified. Incrementalism and decision-making methodologies, implementation and policy, social planning and advocacy planning, a political economy approach, new humanism and pragmatism, have elements which are absent from the procedural technical features of procedural planning theory.[9] The PPT does not put such theories in their proper place. At present, the state of theory in planning is in flux.

There is wide agreement that the PPT requires constant reexamination because it underemphasizes political-organizational and environmental factors.[10] Furthermore, the basic procedural technical tenants of the PPT are viewed as unsatisfactory as regards the application of physical, economic, and social planning. But most relevant to our discussion is the inapplicability of the PPT as a general theory to a system where politics dominates. Any planning theory (or theory in general, for that matter), whether procedural or otherwise, must be measured and judged in terms of comparativeness and applicability: A planning theory would have to include procedural and substantive elements (social, economic, physical planning). The analysis of planning policy set out in the forthcoming chapters does not separate procedure and substance. Procedural features are viewed as being in a state of flux (i.e., depending on systemic, social, structural and political features). Thus, systemic rules of the game, for example, are likely to determine the nature and character of planning organizations, their interactions and procedures. The PPT, perhaps unintentionally, implies a conceptual separation between

4

substantive and procedural knowledge. Furthermore, it assumes rationality (i.e., that there are procedures amenable to assessment of alternatives), and even assumes that there is "one good way."[11] Whether this is correct and applicable to highly politicized systems remains an open research question, which can only be properly answered through comparison.

Observation of real world planning underscores the view that the rationality assumed by the PPT is limited to a narrow domain of procedures, rather than being a guiding concept for planning decisions. The approach adopted here is that issues are made salient during the planning policy decision process through political activity by interested parties. The view that planning alternatives are determined by politics, and not by some assumed rational procedure, clearly suggests that no assumption of rationality as a process which controls the environment and development can be made. Alternatives often emerge as a result of interest or lack of interest in an issue rather than through calculation.[12] A more relevant view of rationality might be that it is an end product related to agreed upon goals.

Some of the major problems that plagued planning theory in the late sixties and the mid-seventies linger on. One key issue is that of diversity in the images and definition of planning as a field of study.[13] In 1977, Galloway and Mahayni issued a call for a theory that would integrate procedural and substantive elements in "ways which reflect the multiplicity of process-object linkage."[14] This theme was later pursued by Paris,[15] and by Healey, McDougall and Thomas.[16] The role of the professional planner was also challenged.

The notion that the bureaucratic planner possesses an acceptable definition of the public interest and can thereby act within his technical field of competence without fearing that his or her activities are the basis for politically intensive group discrimination, has been challenged effectively by the neo-Marxists.[17] The analysis of planning in terms of politics, or more specifically in terms of power relation influence — exchange, negotiation, conflict — should form the basis in the search for a more comprehensive planning theory. Analysis of planning in terms of politics explains much behind planning activity. Blowers stated that "what is required is a theoretical framework which relates the concept of planning to the concept of power...which provides planning with its role, its motivation and its justification."[18]

But political analysis brings with it a number of pitfalls. For example decision analysis often takes for granted issues that are removed from the public agenda. The political analysts must be also cautious about the assignment of power to actors on the basis of single issues. The criteria used to identify active issues and conflicts, the relative impact on outcomes, and the potential and actual exercise of power must also be taken into account.

We are concerned here with discussing planning policy arenas and pointing to the explanatory power of political variables. Our hypothesis is that planning is determined by conflicting actors and organizations, not merely by professional planners. The relative position of each actor and organization is a function of the activation of resource: legal, statutory, organizational, financial and ideological. The approach, whereby planners and their activities were perceived as a technical procedure neutral to power, goals, substance and choice, is no longer acceptable. Planning is choice; it is a goal-setting activity. In a governmental (political) environment these activities emerge as a result of group (or organizational) conflict and its resolution. Even when elites dominate, it is hardly conceivable that no competition is present. Government planning implementation is watchdogged by politicians, hence conflict and correcting steps are likely to emerge. The political roles in planning lead to political determination of planning policy outputs, and in this way the outcomes are legitimized.

The role of overseemanship and legitimization assigned to politics and politicians raises the question about the nature of the relationship between planning and politics. Is it stable or changing in all types of organizational settings and in all types of public issues? A political theory of planning must take into account variations in involvement and political differentiation regarding different public issues. Politicians as decision makers need not always be an integral part of all issues of planning policy making. Their exact role — they can veto, legitimize, delay, ignore, etc. — should be identified empirically. Special attention should be paid to their role in various comparative planning arenas and formal planning-decision organizations.

There have been numerous interpretations of the planning process that underscored the political elements (e.g., the political economy, incrementalization, and decision-making studies), which are distinct positions that take into account conflict and governmental-political variables. These approaches pose a challenge to the PPT. Although Faludi responded to the growing criticism of his PPT by emphasizing policy and political variables such as intensity of control in planning and decisions, the technical nature of the PPT is still paramount.[19] On the other hand, the problem with the various political elements mentioned thus far is that they are not part of an integrated theory of planning politics.

It is evident in planning situations that conflict is pervasive and that its resolution enables the production of planning outputs. Although Faludi recognizes the presence of conflict on the individual level, he disregards the broader view of politics as a regulating and screening process of conflicts. In planning, as in other domains, such conflicts are not just adversary relations between individuals, but real adversary and power relations between the state and urban level over ideology, substance, form, and even over the procedures of how and where policy is conducted. This conception makes planning organizations not a mere procedural tool, but a vehicle of regulation that enables various positions an authoritative outlet.

A political approach to the analysis of planning policy deals with the how and what of planning. Systemic normative features are explicated as part of the conflict resolution process in the planning policy arena. Normative positions of individuals, groups and organizations in planning policy and outcomes are part of planning conflict and its resolution process.

Planning organizations are political (and to a large extent reflect the state's power distribution); they are important in the regulation of conflict and they determine substantive planning. It is not rationality of procedure that is at stake, but rationality in the political sense of goal-oriented action. Such action is achieved when political regulation of conflicts among competing wills is achieved. Planning organization helps give stability to procedure through institutionalized rules and modes of decision. The major emphasis is on organizational political behavior as it determines planning policy and its outcomes.

## The Political Role of Planning Organizations

The political role of planning organizations, as distinct from their technical planning role, has not been sufficiently emphasized in the literature. The analysis adopted here focuses on structural features and the modes of operation of the planning organization, its ability to absorb and regulate conflicts, and the organization's regulative role in routine conditions as well as under conditions of pressure and uncertainty (such as those that prevailed after the 1967 Six Day War, when the city of Jerusalem took responsibility for the Jordanian section). Urban planning organizations under special non-routine conditions are less likely to be able to compete with state organizations and to regulate planning policy conflict than under routine conditions. And because of this they are likely to lose their ability to produce planning-policy.

Focusing on the politics of planning organizations provides the unique opportunity to consider an important variable of politics — namely the preferences and what is valued by different actors and groups. It also touches upon the important question of the nature of group distributional shares in the process of public planning policy. This aspect of planning research has been insufficiently dealt with, especially because advocacy planning research perspectives have been on the wane.[20] Thomas noted: "Rational planning theory represents the technique of continuing progress toward greater benefits for all — untroubled by the question of relative distributional shares.[21]

It is important to identify in planning organizations the parameters of interests, promoters, supporters, and clients of a course of action or policy. The political approach to planning policy subscribes to the view that active, interested parties in planning policy use power and have power relationships.[22] The recognition of interests and power relationships in planning policy indicate a tacit subscription to the pluralist conception of politics. While we recognize a pluralist situation, we certainly do not assume that participants in planning organizations have equal resources, the same capacity, or similar energy to pursue their interests.

Conflict among individuals and organizations in determining planning policy is placed squarely in the central-local relations organizational set — a perspective that is expected to provide a better understanding of the relative weight of influence of various organizations in affecting planning policy and the quality of community life.

## Central-Local Relations of Planning Organizations

The political-conflict framework of central-local relations, which concerns changing networks, contrasts with a definition of the borders of planning policy as clear and hierarchical. The framework of changing networks enables us to deal with different policy situations involving local and central actors and organizations, and draw generalizations about their political relations in different environments, times, and issues. The political analysis of conflict is concerned with what actually occurs in the structural and organizational setting of planning. The bases for explanations lie in the empirical identification of the relative influence of participants in different policy issues and in specific organizational sets. Political analysis also explains the variations in intensity and extent of involvement. The central-local relation perspective enables the identification of the organizational setting of rules of behavior in planning policy. These rules assign roles to various actors and organizations. "Rules carry within themselves implications for who can gain effective access to power within organizations and [are] able to affect organizational policies...."[23] Indeed, the rules that govern central-local relations can be legal or statutory, or informal rules emanating from status acquired through the control of resources.

A variety of models and propositions are available. For Rhodes, the central-local relations of organizations is less one of central control and more of an ambiguous and confused relationship about which neither level of government is clear.[24] He noted two alternatives: the agent and the partnership models. McConaghy spoke of the relations in terms of the extent of centralization and localism.[25] Stanyer discussed the extent of local capacity and autonomy in the light of complex systemic features,[26] which is related to the concept of the local-state.

Whether local government in general is seen as a part of the national system or as more autonomous is, of course, an empirical question. In either case we shall extract from both the national and local systems those actors, organizations, behavior and other elements that are involved in planning policy decisions. By identifying the boundaries of the networks involved in planning policy decisions we adopt a form of a partnership model (albeit not equal and related to structure and power) of urban politics, a procedure I proposed in previous research.[27]

Boyle argues for greater rigor in the research concerning the political approach to planning. He said that "boundaries of decision making at the local scale are crucial."[28] The difference between his boundary notions and the network foci proposed here is that planning policy is dynamic: There are changing networks not only in the real world of planning policy, but also in the very issues and participants within a discernable network; there are identifiable political factors that clarify how and which issues become active and salient; active boundaries for political analysis of planning policy are likely to be established. Lastly, the partnership model is a broad conception. It is not in itself clear about the borders of the partnership and the concomitant networks. It can be labeled as a complex system, similar to the labeling of central-local relations in England by Rhodes.[29] His concept of complexity is not easily operationalized. Nevertheless, we find in Rhodes further support for our model of conflict analysis. He speaks of the need to focus on the bargaining between central and local government, the multiplicity of relationships, and the channels of political and professional influence.[30]

## The Politics of Planning Policy

Analysis of planning policy, and the behavior sets it involves, serve as a basis for making generalizations about the political elements and processes that determine planning policy. The policy perspective and analysis goes beyond a description of professional-technical, and statutory-legal features, to the dynamics of actual behavioral patterns involving the relations of individuals and organizations. Analyzing planning policy with concepts from political behavior analysis allows one to transcend contextual knowledge and move toward propositions with universal application. The analysis of the politics of planning policy behavior enables the exposition of new knowledge about planning. Technical-procedural research emphasis does not divulge such knowledge. An example of this process is the abstraction of knowledge on the basis of political economy paradigms (i.e., that planning policy works in favor of selected interests in society). Clearly, no one approach or set of paradigms explains all the world of planning activity or planning policy. But the set of concepts selected under the political perspective should explain a great deal so that in its absence, or in using an alternative set of paradigms, a gap is discernable regarding the explanation of planning policy.

The following propositions provide a set of statements on the determinants of planning policy:

(1) Structures and rules outline political roles and determine the nature of conflict.

(2) Conflict behavior and its resolution mandates competition and the use of political resources, which aim at using and winning power in an effort to influence or control planning policy.

(3) Individual behavior on behalf of an organization (or profession) aims at exercising influence.

(4) Planning policy issues are activated under a variety of conditions and in changing organizational networks. This involves a multiplicity of individuals and organizations and is the setting for the analysis of the core of the politics of planning policy research: differential power and its use, conflict and its resolution.

There is no one set of agreed definitions of the public interest. Hence, it is unlikely that any one body of people, equipped as they may be with professional credentials, can undertake the sole determination of public policy on behalf of the public interest. The political process is most likely to expose and define a variety of public interests — individual and organizational. Research on planning policy is likely to confirm these pluralistic characteristics of the policy arena or, alternatively, to point to other forms of the translation of public interest to policy decisions. In Israel, structural features of the planning organizations are the setting for an institutional distribution which provides for a definition of the public interest in planning policy. This does not necessarily represent the public at large, rather it reflects the state and urban political distribution of power. Different class participation, and their access to planning policy decisions, is dependent on the general political institutional representative structure. Organized economic and sectorial interests, such as rural landowners and developers, are more likely to find access and expression in the decision arenas of planning policy.

The politics of planning policy is likely to involve issues that cause conflict and confrontation when goals are defined in institutionalized setting (in the planning organizations), when a decision has to be reached, when an exchange situation is likely to lead to conflict resolution, and when the substance of planning policy is non-technical (which is the case with most planning products beyond the drawing table). Political analysis of planning policy explains the competition for dominance present in the process of evolving and implementing planning policy. Political analysis is useful in the understanding of changes that occur in the planners' roles and planning practices. A recent proposition on such changes is: "To maintain a strategic role, at all, they (the planners) are forced to develop capabilities in politics of influence."[31] In the United States and England, comprehensive planning has in part been undermined due to a dominance of an incrementalist conception by Braybrook and Lindbloom. There is an inability to connect comprehensive methodologies to diverse organizations or societies.[32] Concomitantly, incrementalism is humanly and systemically more manageable. And in policy making this is certainly the case. Thus, it may be argued that no professional ambition (for comprehensiveness) or acquired professional position, can come in lieu of the systemic political will. A profession can make only limited claim to represent the public interest. The reality is that any profession is represented by political actors who have a policy arena to struggle for their point of view. The failure of professional bureaucracies to represent the public interest (in the case of the disadvantaged, for example), is evidenced in the widespread demand and advocacy for public participation.

The Israeli setting of planning organizations provides identifiable routes of access to positions of influence; the specific events and relative shares of influence emerge through politics in the various networks of central-local relations. This is discernable in research as well as in the process by which planning policy issues become salient, active, and generate conflict. The core of political analysis is conflict. It involves individuals who may be councilmen, government bureaucrats, planners, developers, and to some limited extent the public. And we shall be explaining their relative capacity to influence policy. Organizations and interest groups have a role in the determination of policy; they are identified in the urban setting as they interact in the national-local political environment of planning policy.

We distinguish between structural policy — the rules and practices that involve (and often assign) political and policy access and roles — and the actual use of the entitlement and access in the pursuit of a planning policy. This will become apparent in the analysis of the planning organizations.[33]

## Planners and Planning Policy

Planning as a profession provides little guidance concerning the professional's behavior within an administrative-political setting and with respect to the type of struggle over goals. Already in 1965, Altshuler asked: "Under what conditions and to what extent should planners dilute the ethic of intellectual honesty to engage in political maneuvers? What sorts of compromises are justifiable? Under what conditions?"[34] Professionally, let alone politically, planners have yet to justify why their point of view is better than others. Assuredly, they can explain the rationale and premises of their position, but to justify them in terms of "better than" is another matter. In early research, Davidoff and Reiner complained about the failure of the training of planners to teach "methods for determining ends...."[35] It is argued here that in the politics of planning policy, a planner's allegiance to his profession is likely to take a back seat to his or her loyalty to the administrative political hierarchy.

The question of the planner's role in planning policy as a political actor often proceeds from the erroneous assumption that he or she has a choice of becoming involved in a planning policy conflict. It is more likely that planners may find themselves involved in a conflict and have to make a choice about their role. In Israel, structural political factors are clearly a determinant of a public planner's choices. The private planning consultants[36] treat their profession as a means of advancing their economic and professional interests.

The planners are for the most part mean-oriented; operational goals are likely to be defined in the broadest terms so that politicians can define them more specifically before or after the plans are submitted. Were planners truly autonomous, the number of encounters with decision makers would be greater than it is. An important function of the public planner is to expose improprieties in administrative procedure, in public bids, and taking part in debates on substantive planning matters. Public planners in Israel may assert professional views within their administrative organization, but they are not likely to assert them outside it nor oppose it. In the actual planning, planners are expected to be constrained by the administrative-political structure. There is little guidance concerning policy role and behavior. The planner, as a professional within an administrative political setting, and with respect to the type of struggle required for long-range goals, acts from within his organization and has many opportunities in asserting a professional point of view. But there are also many limitations and constraints placed upon him by strong mayors and the political environment of planning policy decisions. Given the systemic features, planners in Israel tend to avoid conflict-ridden contests over goals for fear that they might encroach the politician's domain. Consequently, in order to distinguish themselves professionally, planners generally become actors who defer to hierarchy. Inside city hierarchy, a planner cannot be expected to act against the consensus generated by mayoral leadership and Local Planning and Building Commission (LPBC) decisions.

It is argued that planners in Israel have meager opportunities to assert their views beyond the planning organization of which they are a member. The local planners are free to suggest, prepare or generate debate on goals of preferred courses of action. However, they are not free to make their own position public, whether self-appointed or in response to controversial socioeconomic issues, or in response to public opposition. Although a local planner may become involved in a conflict with decision makers, he may do so only within the confines of the local planning arena which, of course, represents the local government political coalition. The organizations, commissions and agencies which have access and a role in planning decisions, represent the ruling local and national political coalition. In this political setting, planners are unable to engage in advocacy planning. They can assert a personal view, but it is likely to lack the status of an independent professional position. In the final analysis the planner is part of the administrative-political hierarchy, and he or she is most likely to serve those in power. The Israeli planner's major clientele is the dominant political coalition and group; he is expected to be accountable to it. Being a part of the administrative-political hierarchy, planners are not likely to speak for the public. Were they elected and thus accountable to the public, they could hold a justifiable position vis-a-vis decision makers. They cannot be expected to serve any clients unless they are part of the administrative-political setting. Their attempts to go public are very likely to be put down. If parties and factions represent various politics, then the interaction that determines goals also reflects various publics. Planners have no public to represent. In Israel the more direct way of representing the public is submerged in as yet unborn future reforms.

Comparing the bureaucrat and planner's discretion during plan preparation it may be expected that they both affect goals, but only indirectly. At this juncture, however, the planning profession has not created the conditions necessary for a planner to be able to choose and define his or her role. At the present time the planner's role must be defined in terms of systemic factors, actors, and the norms of the politico-administrative setting. The profession, in short, cannot be expected to provide guidance to public planners in their role in planning policy conflicts.

# Notes — Chapter 1

1. Saunders, P. *Urban Politics*. London: Hutchison, 1979.
2. Saunders (1979); Castells, M. *The Urban Question*. London, 1977; Arnold, E. and Pahl, R. "Urban Managerialism Reconsidered" in Pahl, R. *Whose City*. London: Longmans, 1977.
3. Lukes, S. *Essays in Social Theory*. London: Macmillan, 1973, p. 29.
4. Saunders (1979), Ch. 1.
5. Healey, P., McDougall G. and Thomas, M.J. *Planning Theory*. Oxford: Pergamon Press, 1982, p. 10.
6. Goldsmith, M. *Politics Planning and the City*. London: Hutchinson, 1980, p. 126.
7. Thomas, M.J. "The Procedural Planning Theory of A. Faludi" in Paris, C. *Critical Readings in Planning Theory*. Oxford: Pergamon Press, 1982, p. 13 and Faludi, A. *Planning Theory*. Oxford: Pergamon Press, 1973.
8. Thomas in Paris (1982), p. 23 and cf. Faludi (1973), p. 296.
9. Healey (1982), p. 6.
10. Healey (1982) and Paris (1982).
11. Paris (1982), p. 5.
12. Thomas in Paris (1982), p. 21.
13. Needleman, M. and Needleman, C.E. *Guerillas in the Bureaucracy*. New York: J. Wiley & Sons, Inc., 1979.
14. Galloway, T.D. and Mahayni, R.G. "Planning Theory in Retrospect: The Process Paradigm Change," *Journal of the American Institute of Planners* 43 (1977):62-71.
15. Paris (1982).
16. Healey, *et al.* (1982), pp. 5-14.
17. Wright, E.O. *Class, Crisis and the State*. London: New Left Books, 1978; Dearlove, J. *The Reorganization of British Local Government: Old Orthodoxies and a Political Perspective*. Cambridge: Cambridge University Press, 1979.
18. Blowers, A. *The Limits of Power: The Politics of Local Planning Policy*. Oxford: Pergamon, 1980, p. 140.
19. Faludi, A. "Toward a Combined Paradigm of Planning Theory" in Paris (1982), p. 31.
20. Gans, H.J. (1986) *People and Plans*, New York: Basic Books, 1986; Davidoff, P. "Advocacy and Pluralism in Planning," *Journal of the American Institute of Planners* 31 (1965):331-8.
21. Thomas, M.J. "The Procedural Planning Theory of A. Faludi," in Paris (1982), p. 24.
22. Blowers, A. "Much Ado About Nothing? A Case Study of Planning and Power" and Boyle, R.M. "Politics and Planning: The Search for a Theory of Influence," in Healey, *et al.* (1982).

23. Dearlove, J. (1979), p. 14.
24. Rhodes, R.A.W. "Some Myths in Central Local Relations," *Town Planning Review* 51 (1980):274, 281-282.
25. McConaghy, D. "Planning in the Critical Decade," *Journal of Town Planning Institute* 67:8-10.
26. Stanyer, J. *Understanding Local Government*. Glasgow: Fontana Press, 1976.
27. Torgovnik, E. "A Perspective on Central Local Relations," *Journal of Comparative Administration* (1972):469-490. See also Alterman, R. "Implementation Analysis in Urban and Regional Planning" in Healey *et al.* (1982), p. 242.
28. Boyle, R.M. in Healey (1982), p. 129.
29. Rhodes, R.A.W. (1980), p. 282.
30. Rhodes, R.A.W. (1980), pp. 273-274.
31. Healey, P., *et al.*, "Theoretical Debate in Planning: Toward a Coherent Dialogue" in Healey, *et al.* (1982), p. 13.
32. Braybrooke, D. and Lindblom, C.E. *A Strategy of Decision*. New York: Free Press of Glencoe, 1973.
33. Ministry of Interior, *Planning and Building Law, 1965*. 4th edition, 5/1985 (Hebrew).
34. Altshuler, A.A. *The City Planning Process: A Political Analysis*. Ithaca: Cornell University Press, 1965, p. 403.
35. Davidoff, P.J. & Reiner, T.A. "A Choice Theory of Planning," *American Institute of Planners Journal* 2 (1962):114; Wright, D.S., "Government Forms and Planning Function: The Relation of Organizational Structures to Planning Practice" in Boyle, T.L. and Lothrop, G.T. *Planning and Politics Uneasy Partners*. New York: Odyssey Press, 1970, p. 69.
36. The professional organization of private planners, which also acts as an interest group, is the Association of Engineers and Architects in Israel.

# Chapter 2

# THE IMPLEMENTATION OF
# URBAN POLICY

This chapter relates the systemic normative features of Israel's urban policy to actual policy implementation. The close link between the central and local settings is revealed from a historical perspective.

The role of government in urban policy means strong, deliberate and often direct interventive action. This was especially the case in the formative years of the state when urban activities were set in motion. Urban policy in Israel is discussed in terms of decisions regarding spatial activity, which reflects structural and normative features and the concomitant policies and strategies it entailed for cities, regions and settlements.

J. Blair and D. Nachmias discuss urban policy in relation to the expanding role of government in programs that relate to urban affairs, to rising needs, and to declining resources.[1] J. Doig and M. Danielson speak of urban growth as an independent variable related to "policies programs and other action of government officials."[2] A broader approach, but one that also reflects a clear stand about a limited regulative role of the government in a market economy, would be where "national urban policy [takes] an entirely new view of functions of cities and of the triadic relationship among deconcentration, private sector development and urban economic welfare."[3]

An urban field may be identified when policy decisions are concerned with (1) major urban and settlement centers; (2) when a system evolves planning policy decision structures; (3) when it is accompanied by controls and support systems that involve resource allocation; and (4) when a difference can be ascertained regarding the extent that the government intervenes in or alternatively leaves such matters to the operation of the market place. For example, a spatial policy involving locational questions of population and urban functions — such as reducing primacy and population dispersal — can be the result of market place choices of individuals or it can be identified as deliberate, systemically controlled planning and implementation of policy involving incentives, support and subsidies.

## Norms, Policies, Strategies and Instruments

Policy, strategy, planning and programs are means that relate to a higher order of societal goals, to definable domains of action, and to a series of implementation instruments (i.e., that urban policy planning can be translated to specific programs). In the United States, for example, urban policy of the 1960s related to equity. It involved measures against poverty and support for weak regions, and thus related policy, planning, strategy and programs to identifiable normative structures. Spatial strategies in Israel are related to identifiable normative features. The question posed here is how are these strategies translated to the means of implementing societal goals?

In Israel these goals are: national security development, absorbing immigrants, controlling allotted and disputed space, and commitment to a high measure of personal equity. Regional equity in Israel may be regarded as a secondary consideration salient with the goals of absorbing immigrants and controlling the use of space. There is, in general, a hierarchy of concepts from societal goals to policy, to strategy, and lastly to the program level. Each element of the hierarchy is likely to have its own goals, but in the final analysis these goals are but a link between the hierarchical elements. According to H.W. Richardson, spatial goals "are not ends but means, i.e., ways of using spatial reorganization as a means of achieving the higher level societal goals."[4]

The framework of themes that will dominate the present discussion relates to an infrastructure of various policy elements that are required in order to facilitate and achieve the realization of goals. These policy elements are political commitment, ordered planning and implementation procedures, identifiable procedures of control, and ordered resource allocation (which includes incentives and subsidies). These elements are universal; they can be applied to systems other than Israel. The elements thus have comparative implications, although no comparisons with other systems are attempted here.

Political commitment, in the form of political support within the administrative structure, is the first necessity. The other three policy elements are really implementation instruments.

Instruments of implementation vary. No single theory can help determine the appropriateness of instruments. Each national setting is likely to vary in the selection of instruments; the presence of similar tools in different political systems is not excluded. For example, there can be much similarity of difference in the implementation instruments of new towns policy in Israel and England. In England new towns can be privately initiated, while in Israel, however, the implementation strategies differ greatly as to what societal goals are to be served.[5]

Control and support of a policy follows a political decision. The policy may involve: (1) new modes of implementation and administrative structures; (2) the use of extensive planning; and (3) a differential incentive support and subsidy system. Control of a policy can be identified when the implementation structure possesses mechanisms of correction.[5]

After discussing some general features of national urban policy in Israel, five major areas of policy will be investigated in terms of the policy element framework: Rural and urban planning; population dispersal; stability and change in new towns; the regulation of land and population movement; and neighborhood renewal. The emphasis, in terms of length, devoted to the five topics is somewhat uneven and reflects the historical perspective devoted to each topic.

## General Features of National Urban Policy

Active Zionism dates back to the last decade of the nineteenth century. It has always been involved with the movement of populations, settlements, and development. These activities reflected identifiable normative features and were directed by national, political, and administrative centers.

In 1922, 83,000 resided in what was then called Palestine. A third lived in the Tel Aviv district and vicinity. In 1948, the population was 717,000; in 1951, 1,404,000; and in 1957, 1,763,000. Between 1948 and 1951 the population doubled. (By comparison the Jewish population had doubled between 1922 and 1931, and tripled between 1931 and 1944.)[6]

Urban strategy in Israel involves intervention decisions; Israel has only moderately gone for the market option. The exception is the policies toward big cities (Tel Aviv and Jerusalem) up to 1948, when the State of Israel was established. Up to this time the ruling institutions took these urban centers for granted. The cities were left to develop through market force and were neglected. This was in sharp contrast to the rural section, which was planned, directed and enjoyed high status. After 1948, however, a new towns development policy received much national attention and resources.

The establishment of the State of Israel in 1948 did not diminish the dominant rural ideology, but the nature of settlement patterns and planning changed. The doubling of the population and the continued plans to absorb immigrants posed new and unexpected pressures on governing bodies. Israel willingly absorbed survivors of the Holocaust and others who left Arab and North African countries in the wake of the Arab-Israel conflict. This influx of people dictated events and the result was a new urban orientation and a strategy of new towns. The masses of new immigrants were not directed to existing cities.

Israel was concerned with the security and control of newly acquired (disputed) territories; hence the strategy of population dispersal. The existing *kibbutzim* (collective settlements) and *moshavim* (semi-private settlements) were closed socioeconomic units that chose not to expand or change their monastic, ideologically homogeneous character despite demands that they absorb new immigrants. Being an important part of the ruling Labor party they were able to resist pressure for change. Given their own outstanding example they argued for dispersal — pioneering in remote places — as they themselves had done in the past. Moreover, it is doubtful whether the bulk of the new immigrants were inclined to a collectivist type of living. The majority were from a traditional background. Their emphasis was on the family and familial authority. They were estranged from socialism, the dominant ideology in the formative years. Immigrants who came from urban centers in Europe, Asia and Africa were largely alien to rural living.

Despite out-migration because of the unattractiveness and remoteness of the new towns, and the stigma attached to some of them, they nevertheless signified a major change in Israel's urban policy and planning outlook.[7] Their establishment made inroads into the agrarian emphasis and polar model of planning. (The polar model was supported by those whose political allegiance was to the ideological, rural framework, which did not provide for intermediate size towns in the hinterland.) The new hierarchical spatial planning model was a familiar concept to those versed in European planning. The hierarchical model decentralized activities to the regions in the form of rural village settlements, rural centers (population up to 1,000), rural-urban centers (population up to 12,000), medium-sized towns as regional centers for the lesser settlements (population up to 70,000) and, lastly, large urban centers.

The new towns policy was followed by a major institutional planning reform, the "Planning and Housing Law, 1965" (PHL 1965). Agrarianism was also entrenched formally by clauses relating to the preservation of agricultural lands in this law, which became the major tool of regulation of open land use. What contributed to the acceptance of the new towns policy among the political leadership was the compound structure of ideology and new national goals. With the establishment of the state there was the need to control disputed areas, coupled with a belief in the lasting political effect of a physical presence in the newly acquired land. Concomitant with this was a psychological factor. The waves of immigration in the early 1950s, and the potential Jewish immigrants from Russia and western countries, created rising expectations, which in turn, created political support for new, bold policies. The attraction to the political elite of the planners' hierarchical new towns structure was the population dispersal of the wave of immigration.

E. Brutzkus, who had a key role in planning in the early years, has reported that Prime Minister Ben-Gurion personally ordered the acceptance of the hierarchical model, which became the basis for the new towns policy of rural-urban centers and middle-size towns.[8] The budget gave expression to the new towns and dispersal policies. Planners in the government, the Jewish Agency, and various settlement research centers, became geared to the new planning concept. One administrative interventive technique was the formation of settlement teams that followed the program of the establishment of towns. M. Aronoff studied how this was done in the new town of Arad, in the Negev. The implementation team constantly had to negotiate for resources with the fractionalized government system of competing ministries. That they, and eventually the local government, were able to do this with some measure of success is indicative of the whole process of settlement politics.

## Rural and Urban Policy

Prior to the establishment of Israel, the Jewish governing institutions in Palestine produced an impressive array of planned settlement programs. After 1948 these programs were linked to the effort of development and nation building. A similar linkage took place in urban policy. Common to both development and urban policy is the deliberateness of resource allocation and the controls used to implement it. An important distinguishing factor between the two activities and periods lies in the underlying planning conception. Before the establishment of the state, the idealized rural sector received preference in budget allocations (Table 2.1).

Table 2.1

PARTIAL EXPENDITURE OF JEWISH INSTITUTIONS
BY SECTOR, 1921-1937

| Purpose | Pounds Sterling (thousands) | Percentage |
|---|---|---|
| Agricultural Settlement | 2,055 | 34 |
| Immigration | 716 | 11.9 |
| Urban Settlement | 481 | 8 |

Source: World Zionist Federation Executive and Jewish Agency Executive, Report for the 20th World Zionist Congress, p. 234.

Note: Expenditures for housing and culture not included. Figures relate only to the expenditure of Keren Hayesod, the building organ of the Jewish Agency.

At the 13th World Zionist Congress held in Carlsbad, it was decided that 30 percent of the budget would be allocated to agriculture. This preference was of long standing.[9] Some of the American and European branches of the 13th Congress raised the question of the importance of urban expenditures and succeeded in passing a resolution that recommended, in vague terms, that the Jewish National Fund allocate land not only to agriculture but also to housing in cities for new immigrants.[10] However, the Labor section, representing those who actually lived in Palestine, determined the activities, which were focused on the rural sector.

The early preference for the rural sector was an outcome of the Zionistic ideological framework that viewed the return to the land as the core of national revival. The Jewish governing institutions were guided by this ideology. There were also more prosaic reasons for ruralism. Zionism was concerned with acquiring legitimacy over the land; a physical presence was thus an important element of nationalism. A. Rupin, who was in charge of channelling the resources of world Jewry to Palestine, made this point clear by noting that "agriculture helped colonization," by which he meant the legal acquisition of land.[11]

Two other aspects require elaboration concerning the pre-state period. The first deals with the setting for the dominant ideology, and the second with the relative neglect of urban places by the national governing institutions. The example of the city of Tel Aviv is a case in point. By 1933 it had grown to a population of nearly 80,000 against the background of an anti-city ideology and an elite bent on not supporting city life. Paradoxically, at a time when rural pioneerism was a national ideology, it was the urban center of Tel Aviv that was the focus for all economic activity, trade and industry. Political institutions, newspapers and many of the leaders who carried the torch of ruralism, were located in the city. The mass of middle class immigrant absorption took place in the city. Between 1922 and 1929, for example, most immigrants had urban occupations; they were not inclined to rural living. Their enterprise gave Tel Aviv its economic thrust. The socialization of some of the new immigrants to the very notions of rural pioneerism also took place in the city. Faced with these unstoppable trends, the Labor elite forged the Histadrut Labor Federation. The Histadrut was instituted on collectivist lines. The idea was to embrace the urban masses of immigrants, mobilize them, and to some extent, deliver them from the evils of city life. The Labor Federation was not a mere trade union but an organization deeply involved in members' lives. Collective resources were used to accommodate individual needs; the federation provided work, indoctrination into socialist ideals, housing, education, and health care.

The political power acquired by the Labor elite[12] at this time resulted from their ability to present themselves as the spokesmen of the Jewish population in Palestine, both rural and urban.

Skillfully controlling national and world Jewry[13] resources, the Labor party mobilized masses of urban immigrants with non-rural inclination to the rural ideology.

The pre-state period was characterized by a lack of urban planning, which had a negative effect in terms of societal goals. Israel's new towns could not answer the needs of the waves of immigrants. Although about 20 percent of the immigrants did settle the new towns, many continued to be accommodated in temporary dwellings close to the cities — areas that later turned into centers of poverty and slums. Even in the 1980s, two cities adjacent to Tel Aviv, Bat Yam and Holon, were still looking for urban solutions to two of these early transient camps.

An illustrative example of the freedom to ignore urban needs in specific cases was the persistent resistance of Ben-Gurion, and later Dayan, concerning the planning of Ramat Aviv, a Tel Aviv suburb. It was first designated as agricultural land. To give more credence to their inclinations, they put forward security reasons as the need for population dispersal. Ramat Aviv has since evolved as one of the most expensive urban neighborhoods in Israel. Applying planning skills to the rural sector produced a network of rural settlements and a thriving agriculture, but it was at the expense of the city. Cohen argues that the neglect of the city was detrimental to the declared Labor goals of national development, as it is inconceivable to think of modernization without cities.[14] Tel Aviv grew through market forces, neighborhood by neighborhood, but it lacked an urban concept. The city even reflected a political cleavage: mayors have been mostly from the center-right parties, while up to 1977 national politics was dominated by the center-left.

## Ruralism as Personal Redemption

The discussion of urban and rural planning must be put into a broader perspective. It was no surprise that Zionism viewed the return to the land as a redeeming process. In the European diaspora, Jews were not as a rule allowed to own land. Their concentration in ghettos made for a closed economy. According to Sloski, in the mid and late nineteenth century, the occupation structure of Jews in Europe was about a third in inn-keeping and housing, another third in trade, over a sixth in artisanship, and only one percent in farming. Sloski's categorization leaves out the "camouflage" professions, known in Yiddish folklore as *luft-geschften*, meaning literally "trading in air" and implying an unstable ephemeral type of earning one's living. In comparison, 24 percent of the Jews in Palestine in 1944 were occupied in agriculture.[15] Dreams of change were linked to land ownership. Jewish movements in Eastern Europe, such as BILU (1890-1900), formed the *moshavot* — semi-agricultural towns based on private entrepreneurship. The land as a source of livelihood and personal redemption thus had very early roots.

Borochov,[16] a socialist writer and intellectual who adopted Marxian and Tolstoyan ideas, spoke about the lopsided pyramid of the Jewish occupational structure. He argued for the creation of a pyramid whose broad base is the land. Providing impressive statistics that showed the low percentage of Jews in agriculture at the turn of the century (Germany, 1.3 percent; the U.S. 10 percent; Russia about 4 percent), Borochov concluded that the more a profession is removed from nature, the greater the number of Jews. The ideas advocated by Borochov and his contemporaries became the ideological foundation for collective cooperative ownership of economic enterprises and rural settlements.

The glorification of land and work is identified in Israel with A.D. Gordon.[17] According to Gordon, man actualizes himself through working on the land. Gordon's example, in the form of the first kibbutz, Degania, was much emulated. B. Katznelson, the much admired labor leader and ideologue, argued that land has a rehabilitating capacity. Although he settle himself in a kibbutz near Degania, he also helped to organize urban masses and to build the Histadrut complex in the city.[18]

During the fourth major wave of immigration to Palestine (1924-29), labor leaders realized that city needs had to be coped with. Over 60,000 persons arrived, mainly from Poland, escaping anti-Jewish policies of the Polish government. These immigrants differed from the earlier pioneers. They were mostly tradesmen and craftsmen, and they possessed some capital. Many of these immigrants could have emigrated elsewhere, but the U.S. was blocked by restrictions. Palestine was viewed as a place to live in but not necessarily as a national mission. Indeed, when hardships and recession occurred, 25,000 of them left. Non-socialist leaders, such as M. Dizengoff, lamented their absence because the capital they had brought with them was no longer available for investment in the city. Those who remained stayed mainly in the cities and became politically influenced by the rural collectivist ideology. According to D. Giladi, they perceived their stay in the city as a deviation from the idealized image.[19]

Despite a reduction in the percentage of the population in the rural sector from 25 percent in 1945 to about 9 percent in 1980,[20] the high status of the rural sector did not diminish in terms of its political strength within the Labor party and the Histadrut. By the 1980s the kibbutzim and moshavim had adjusted to technological change; they now use their collective status to achieve economic might through industrial enterprises and modernized agriculture. In 1984, the production value of the kibbutzim rose by 10 percent compared with 1983 and was around one billion dollars.[21]

The historic momentum and continuation of Jews seeking to acquire land continued in the 1980s. But now it is the center-right political movement that champions the cause, not Labor. Moreover, there is much debate as to Israel's right to settle in the controversial areas of the West Bank and Gaza. Whether the settlement policy and activity is as appropriate now as it was in the past is open to question. But in both instances, certain dimensions of policy can be discerned: central decisions, national resource allocation, and various features of control.

## The Role of Central Authorities

The brief historical note above, and the sections below that deal with urban policies in the post-state period, place the matter of national urban policy as an important undertaking of the Zionist revolution. In both periods central authorities played a key role. Their current role is briefly considered before analyzing specific policies.

Up to the late 1920s the authorities in the form of world Jewish organizations played a major role in settlement policies. Since the early 1930s, however, an indigenous central authority emerged in Palestine. This authority enjoyed wide support from world Jewish organizations, but the latter were clearly subservient to it. The center's capacity to determine policy became dominant when the State of Israel was established, at which time processes of development, urbanization and modernization received further momentum.

Local government in Israel since 1948 has increased in scope and in the intensity of its activities, but has gradually been weakened in the capacity to finance itself. In the early 1950s, local government in Israel financed about 65 percent of the education budget. In the 1980s its share is about 35 percent. The government evolved a network of administrative, financial and policy links to single settlements, whether through its regional offices or directly. At the same time, strong political parties made further links with national and local authorities. The major policies of settlement and absorption of immigrants were determined by the central government; and major resource mobilization and taxation remained in the hands of the central authorities. Implementation, however, involves the local level. Disagreement and conflict is worked out through negotiation and bargaining between the single local community and a government ministry. The results of negotiations are not always predictable. Clearly, in a unitary system such as Israel's, there is strong central potential for intervention, especially through rule making. Yet, the democratic nature of government allows for various avenues of expression at the local level. A fruitful way to view the central-local relationship is through the following conceptualization: both levels of government act in different policy issues with different motivations and varied aspirations of control of the issue at hand. This pattern was noted in the issue of the location of power stations.[22]

The pattern of central-local relations resulted in: (1) an increased policy-making capacity at both national and local levels; (2) continuous interaction between central and local governments, with varied degrees of institutionalization; (3) structured arenas of policy competition, such as the local, regional and national planning organizations; and (4) a constant change in roles and scope of activities. The role of central government is rarely purely hierarchical in relation to local government. The role of central vis-a-vis local government in urban matters is dominant in some policy areas, but often it is minor and one can almost always view the relationship as a shared responsibility that is interactive, cooperative, competitive, and which involves varied stakes, resources, commitment and exchange procedures. Political developments influenced both central and local governments and their relationships. Growing political self-rule of local governments emerged at a time when national parties became weaker and sometimes even stagnant. This change persisted in spite of the aforementioned financial weakening of local governments. Central tutelage over local governments is on the wane due to (a) the universalization of procedures and removal to a great extent of political considerations in resource allocation; (b) the institutionalization of allocation rules; and (c) the emergence of indigenous assertive local leadership. The only major democratic structural reform to take place in Israel was at the local level: since 1978 mayors have been elected locally.

The central-local partnership that emerged was the setting for at least three major policy proposals: (1) metropolitan reforms, which would include streamlining of services and government structure in the major urban regions of Israel; (2) the level of government financial support to major local government services was placed at a universal roof of 75 percent of the cost of nationally sponsored or approved services, thus providing for a policy of redistribution; and (3) the effort to redefine central-local relations constitutionally and financially through a national commission for local government affairs (the Sanbar Reform Commission).[23] Of these three policies, only the second was implemented. Efforts at structural reform are still on the public agenda, although many features of the proposed reforms have been implemented in a piecemeal manner. For example, the Sanbar Commission argued for clear standards and criteria for the allocation of government funds to local communities. Progressively, each local unit receives welfare and education resources on the basis of clear allocation factors (per capita, community wealth). The Ministry of Interior now provides for a redistributive balancing grant to achieve a minimum service level to all.

In the early years of the state, the role of the center was more dominant in the policies of population dispersal, new towns policies, and other activities. These are discussed in subsequent sections below.

## Population Dispersal

Dispersal policy has a positive ring to it. It hints at the popular notion of getting away from primacy with deliberateness. Dispersal, when actualized, can take different forms, such as the fostering of secondary cities, regional subsystems, a development axis, new towns, and numerous other options. A number of major features stand out in relation to population dispersal in Israel.

First, primacy was viewed as negative, and with good reason. Up to 1948, the Jewish settlements and populations were unevenly distributed. In 1936, 36.35 percent of the population resided in Tel

Aviv and over 42 percent in its vicinity (by 1947 the latter yardstick was 55 percent).[24] Second, there was a dominant notion that it was possible for the government to disperse populations using planning tools and implementation measures. Third, the fact that Israel was a willing host and ready to absorb waves of immigrants made it almost self-evident that the dispersal of people was possible. Fourth, notions of a market that regulates locational matters were excluded from the decision arena. Most newly-arrived immigrants were, as the common Hebrew word *klita* indicates, absorbed by state-run bodies. Lastly, dispersal was viewed as contributing to the widely agreed upon notion of state security, safe borders, and control of space and territory.

The instruments to implement dispersal were readily available. There was a will to settle and develop the newly established state. The notion of Israel as a melting pot for Jews from different countries created an excitement. A sense of legitimacy for state intervention in peoples' lives was built up during the pre-state years of socialist leadership. Consequently, the early years of nationhood gave the leadership much freedom. The relative poverty of most of the immigrants who arrived in Israel in the first decade and a half of its existence contributed to the emergence of various tools of managing people. When the government established the famous *maabarot* transit camps and settlements, it could locate them with relative freedom in remote places, near the agriculturally developed settlements or near the big cities where some employment was available. By the time programs for new towns were undertaken, dispersal policy was a widely accepted societal goal that encompassed control of the territories and guided economic development (until today new towns are called development towns).

Slowing down primacy through population dispersal may be viewed as both an urban policy and a normative stand against city life, whose evils allegedly plagued the Jewish people in the diaspora.[25] The targets set by the statutory plans for the country's population dispersal are a measurement of the success or failure of the policy. This is true for the aggregate measures of people per region, or for people per city. (The relative effectiveness of the various dispersal tools will not be measured here, however.)

The implementation process of the population dispersal policy involved: (1) planning, (2) a system of incentives used to persuade people to relocate at the more distant places, and (3) the deliberate and controlled relocation of poor immigrants to specific locations.

The combination of outright intervention and subsidization is in itself interesting, but was it successful? (Were the goals of dispersal achieved?) This is of particular importance because what lurked strongly behind the deliberate intervention efforts was an open locational market where private choices could be made, especially during periods of economic prosperity. The dynamics involved in the first and third instruments, the planning process and the direction of people away from primacy, are considered here. The second instrument, the process of incentives, is considered in the following section on the new towns. A word of caution is necessary, however. In the scope of this chapter it is not possible to refine aggregate data on population locations and to ascertain who went where and why. The most that can be achieved is the explication of a pattern, and in this vein migration balances will be indicated. The variables contributing to individual choice to move away from nationally preferred locations is discussed in the section on new towns.

## Plans of Dispersal

The deliberate efforts to disperse population are attested to by the fact that since 1949, a year after the establishment of the State of Israel, seven national plans of population dispersal were prepared by the Ministry of Interior on behalf of the government. The 1949 plan was targeted for two million people, the 1951-52 plan for 2.7 million, the 1954 plan for 3.3 million, the 1957-58 plan for 4 million, and the same in 1963 and 1967. In 1972 the plan foresaw five million people in the various regions by the year 1992. An interim report of the 1972 plan foresaw four million people in 1981.[26] A new plan for the year 2010 foresees 7 million people in Israel.

All plans prior to and including the 1972 plan were similar in a number of respects: (1) although the plans had no legal status, they were prepared and implemented by professional planners within the Ministry of Interior; the planners had access to planning and regulating organs such as the regional planning commissions, and in this way were able to influence population dispersal decision; (2) dispersal plans were only formally adopted after a period of trial and error; (3) the prevalence of the normative features previously elaborated, and the high legitimacy of intervention, helped to create a high degree of integration in the actual implementation.

Dispersal policies were aided by two major factors — first, the availability of abandoned Arab neighborhoods and towns in various locations provided places for settlers; second, deliberate planning efforts, such as took place in the Lachish region. These two factors, aided by a huge national commitment of resources, contributed to slowing down primacy. The Lachish region development was a concrete planning effort. It was not only a secondary growth center, but was also juxtaposed to the regional development program of Beersheba, a former Arab town and colonial regional capital. The plans prior to 1972 helped to create a network of settlements that by 1972 were existent and which the 1972 plan took into account and projected into the 1990s. Stated differently, the 1972 plan can be said to have taken into account past deeds as given constraints and hence projected growth using a given growth setting.

## Effectiveness of Dispersal

Population dispersal is a formally adopted program that meets the criteria of an effective policy instrument. It involves national allocational resources, a high degree of control, and correcting mechanisms in the statutory implementation tools at the local, regional and national levels, together with relative freedom to use incentives and subsidies. The actual effectiveness of population dispersal may be defined as the net movement of actual populations in the various preferred region notwithstanding market forces and private choices. In measuring the effectiveness there is a hidden assumption that some regions were less attractive than others when measured against private choices.

Of the immigrants (excluding prior populations) that arrived in Israel between 1961 and 1972, 28 percent went initially to the southern region, 20 percent to the north, and 19.5 percent to the central region. The Tel Aviv region received 12.9 percent of the immigrants, Haifa received 15.2 percent, and Jerusalem 6.8 percent.[27] The data indicate that, at least initially, the settlement of people met some criteria of effective distribution. The most dramatic change of population was in the relatively arid southern region. Between 1948 and 1961 the relative percentage share (in terms of population) of this region grew from 0.9 percent to 8 percent. The central region also shows growth from 15.2 percent in 1948 to 19.7 percent in 1972. The primacy area of the Tel Aviv region had 43.2 percent in 1948; in 1972 it held the share of only 33.5 percent (Table 2.2).

Table 2.2

JEWISH POPULATION DISTRIBUTION BY REGION,
1948-1981 (in thousands)

| Region | 1948 (%) | 1961 (%) | 1972 (%) | 1981 (%) |
|---|---|---|---|---|
| Jerusalem | 84.2 (12) | 187.7 (9.7) | 261.1 (9.7) | 335.3 (10.1) |
| North | 53.4 (7.6) | 194.3 (10) | 255.7 (9.5) | 322.0 (9.7) |
| Haifa | 147.7 (21.1) | 322.3 (16.7) | 408.8 (15.2) | 464.8 (14) |
| Center | 106.2 (15.2) | 380.1 (19.7) | 535.3 (19.9) | 743.7 (22.4) |
| Tel Aviv | 302.1 (43.2) | 692.6 (35.9) | 892.9 (33.5) | 92.7 (29.9) |
| South | 6 (.9) | 155.3 (8) | 323.8 (12.1) | 434.9 (13.1) |
| West Bank | — — | — — | 1.5 (.1) | 23.2 (.7) |
| TOTAL | 699.6 (100) | 1,932.3 (100) | 2,679.1 (100) | 3,320.3 (100) |

Source: *Statistical Yearbook of Israel*, 1983, p. 33 and Benvenisti.

Since 1972 it has been possible to make more specific comparisons in relation to approved statutory plans. Table 2.3 enables a comparison of the actual population distribution in the regions for 1972 and 1981, against the 1972 population dispersal plan (approved in 1975), which is the long range plan for 1992. Comparison will enable us to ascertain the net effectiveness of the dispersal policy. The most striking difference is found in the central region. The 1972 plan foresaw an 18.8 percent share. By 1981 the share was 22.4 percent at the expense of the Tel Aviv region. The plan has not achieved its aim of decreasing the relative share of the center region, which is attractive as individual choice. In the Jerusalem region, the 1.4 percent difference between the projected and actual means that the target to increase the Jewish population of Jerusalem compared with the Arab population has not been met. In Tel Aviv, the aim of decreasing the scope of primacy was moderately accomplished, mainly because of the high cost of living in the center city location and various urban problems. Suburbanization reduced the population of the center of the city out toward the surrounding towns.

Table 2.3

COMPARISON OF JEWISH POPULATION DISTRIBUTION BY REGION: 1972 PROJECTION COMPARED WITH ACTUAL 1981 POPULATION

| Region | 1972 Population Projection | | Actual 1981 Population | |
|---|---|---|---|---|
| | Total Pop. | Jewish Pop. | Total Pop. | Jewish Pop. |
| Jerusalem | 12.6% | 11.5% | 11.5% | 10.1% |
| North | 15.7 | 10.1 | 15.8 | 9.7 |
| Haifa | 15.2 | 14.6 | 14.3 | 14.0 |
| Center | 17.4 | 18.8 | 20.3 | 22.4 |
| Tel Aviv | 26.9 | 31.1 | 25.2 | 29.9 |
| South | 12.2 | 13.2 | 12.2 | 13.1 |
| West Bank | – | .7 | – | .7 |
| Total Population (in thousands) | 3,970.5 | 3,378.0 | 3,977.9 | 3,320.3 |

Source: *Five Million Distribution Plan*, Planning Division, Central Bureau of Statistics, Jerusalem (July 1972). See also *City and Region* (Jerusalem: 1972-3).

The dispersal of population involves complex factors such as development, housing, education, individual choice, and deliberate government action. Although the government was successful in settling the southern region, it was less able to control individual choice and growth in the central region. Measuring the success of population dispersal thus requires a broader perspective than sheer statistical data. Another factor lies in the projections themselves. S. Reichman rightly notes that population projections were not always in tune with economic growth projections and hence there was little coordination between different government ministries.[28]

Another important factor behind the projections is the assumption that the government acts in concert and with coordination. This assumption is highly questionable given the confederated structure of the Israeli government and experience prior to the 1972 plan. Although the government does have plans of dispersal, its control of individual choice and economic activity is less than would be necessary for meaningful population dispersal according to the plans. For example, a firm's decision on location involves factors such as the availability of skilled manpower, the closeness to technology and research, etc. These factors counteract the government's efforts to draw firms to remote places through tax incentives and subsidies. Furthermore, the plans were expected to guide national and local planning and government action, but in the light that the plans did not induce any sort of coherent comprehensive government implementation policy, it was only to be expected that deviations would occur. For example, because in primacy regions the economic activity is strong, it is not likely that the regions will lose their preeminence. The government attempted to offset the high cost to firms in the primacy regions through giving subsidies to firms in other regions, but this can only be partially successful. Government control in a mixed economy can be expected to be effective on a project level, or on a single town level, but it is much less successful within the context of a comprehensive national policy.

## Stability and Change in New Towns

Since the inception of the new towns policy in Israel, research has been concerned with the outcome of this planning effort. Beyond professional questions such as site location, the social profile of the populations, the economic base, primacy vs. periphery, etc., research has focused on the question of the success of the development towns.[29] Success was measured around in- and out-migration and its net effect in terms of the number of people in a given town (a measurement concept much favored by geographers). The in- and out-population measure suffers from certain shortcomings. For example, the measure takes no account of the types of populations and the social-economic forces that affect group cohesion. It is not surprising, therefore, that the success of the new towns policy has been discussed indirectly in terms of population dispersal. This was done, for example, by A. Shachar and S. Reichman.[30] Measuring the success of a specific town is, of course, beyond the scope of a chapter on national urban policy. Needless to say it involves complex procedures. My concern here is with the new towns policy as a reflection of a deliberate national activity that involves resource allocation and control. Let us therefore relate the in-out migration issue to the government's ability to control.

In the democratic milieu of Israel, the continuous control of people and their place of settlement can only be indirect, through incentives and subsidies. Beyond these tools, Israel was and remains an open market for individual choice. True, some of the incentives for people to remain in development towns are highly attractive: low rent, individual tax concessions, low cost loans to individuals and businesses, etc. However, the direct control of people's location (toward new towns) existed only initially, at a time when the masses of immigrants arrived with no capital or familiarity with the system. These people were indeed directed and physically delivered to the more remote settlements. Their towns were often run by government-appointed officials, and the inhabitants' livelihood often depended on government-sponsored work projects.[31]

The new towns policy aimed at changing the settlement mosaic in Israel. The southern region, for example, was sparsely populated with agricultural settlements. By 1955, thirteen new towns had been established there. Between 1950 and 1951 alone, the government allocated resources for five new towns. The peak of the national effort was in 1964 when twenty-seven new towns could be counted, as well as an additional eight as a result of abandoned Arab towns.[32] This deliberate national effort emerged against a background of long-standing experience with the planning and establishment of agricultural settlements and the urgent need to settle newly arrived immigrants. The development towns emerged as either rural centers or regional towns. From the outset the planning conception designated them as service locations, and trade and small industry centers. This planning conception implicitly assumed continued government tutelage, support and control until an assumed take off would occur. The new towns were innovative not so much in the planning conception they represented, but in their deviation from the dominant ruralism and practice that had previously dominated planning ideology.

Another novel feature was that the new towns policy — along with the establishment of new agricultural settlements — dispersed population and broke down the basic polarized structure of the pre-state period in which nearly 60 percent of the Jewish population lived in the urban centers of Tel Aviv, Haifa and Jerusalem. The new towns were the first major effort in national urbanization (apart from the traditional centers of the three major cities which, to a large extent, had evolved by market mechanisms). This deliberate urbanization effort is clearly identifiable by the fact that by 1980, new towns accounted for nearly 20 percent of the population.[33]

Ongoing evaluation of the new towns policy resulted in a variety of correcting programs involving housing for the young, the moving of public institutions to new towns, and continuous assessment of their economic and social performance. Some results of this national evaluation were: (1) the establishment of a special office to encourage professionals from primacy area to move to new towns, by providing incentives; (2) designation of the new towns on a scale of need and providing corresponding subsidies to the local government, individuals, and entrepreneurs; (3) organization of a subsidized service delivery system that assured a minimum level of services; (4) preference as regards special community services and educational programs. The housing element, within the subsidized service delivery system, is the most costly. The centralized programs of housing enable a measure of equity to take place within the context of different costs of construction.

National policies do not imply concerted action. Ministries in Israel represent a political coalition mosaic. They often act as a confederation; administrative coordination of field activities is weak. This affects the ability to act from the center and directs policy decisions of the government as a whole. For example, in three development towns, calculation showed that creating a communication axis between the towns and the regional centers would improve the towns' social networks. However, the Ministry of Construction and Housing expected the budgets to come from the Ministry of Transport, which had its own priorities in different towns.[34] These types of problems, however, pose a difficulty for all settlements in Israel, including the large cities, and not merely for the new towns.

National control is also facilitated by political development in the new towns. Places that were managed by central political agents in the early 1950s are managed in the 1980s by highly politicized local leaderships. Contrary to national Israeli politics, the political leadership in the new towns is young. These highly socialized leaders use the system to deliver resources to their towns that might have been lost in the national administrative bureaucratic maze.[35] For example, the mayor of the town of Yavneh, through sheer skill and political acumen, succeeded in rapidly mobilizing the resources due his town for neighborhood renewal. Thus, his political skills and activities rationalized government action.

## Control Through Subsidies and Incentives

Subsidies and incentives are key instruments in implementing a national urban policy. The most recent example of such implementation is in the West Bank, where scores of new towns and cities were established between 1977 and 1984, and previously from 1968. The government assured the growth of these regions by direct full financing, comprehensive planning and implementation, by providing an elaborate infrastructure and communications network, and through financial incentives and subsidies to individuals and firms. The pattern was not new. Setting aside unique features such as ideology, political factors and involvement of the military, it was similar in the implementation of urban policy in new towns inside the pre-1967 Israel borders.

Some examples will illuminate the scope of the system of supports. In a Ministry of Construction and Housing publication that lists the various loans and subsidies available for housing, a word of caution appears: "In no case shall the overall loans exceed 95 percent of the cost of the apartment.[36] A second example is even more illuminating. Each town has a list of subsidies and supports that are available. In one set of supports for residents of 24 "development settlements," as the ministry refers to them, 20 percent of the personal loan is not linked to a cost of living index — and this at a time when inflation was advancing at 500 percent per year (November 1983). The result is that about 8 percent of the cost of the apartments are practically a direct additional subsidy. In the West Bank area, the subsidies are even higher because the cost of infrastructure is often not included in the price of housing.

National control of policy through incentives and subsidies takes other forms. A variety of government corporations provide low cost financing to entrepreneurs. Tourism projects, for example, can be undertaken in selected new towns as well as in other places. A more direct system of incentives and grants encouraging investment in development towns is made through the national investment law. The preamble to the law reads as follows: "The purpose of the law is to attract capital to Israel, encourage economic initiatives and investments...in order to...absorb immigration, [and make a] proper division of the population over the entire area of the state, and create new places of work."[37] This broad description addresses itself to population dispersal and new towns policies. The law provides for a long list of subsidies, tax incentives and grants to investors.

One outcome of this law has been a system of classifying the development towns on a scale of privileges. The government defines weak and strong towns, and places those which it wishes to "prefer" in its supports. This indeed is an awesome tool of development control. In assessing this law evaluation should be made more in terms of its effectiveness in mobilizing capital and less in terms of what supports it provides. The fact remains that in one town an investor will receive more incentives and in another less. This situation has created "politics of classification." Towns fight hard for the coveted A+, which is the highest level of support. For example, Upper Nazareth and Migdal Ha'emek, two development towns in the Galilee, were recently reclassified by the national budget division in the Treasury as development region B. In previous years, they were classified as A, and each year the Ministry of Industry and Trade would appeal for their reclassification. In 1984 they were refused the A classification.

Inter-ministerial conflict over the right to determine policy provokes strong responses. The director of the Ministry of Industry and Trade reacted to the changed classification by arguing that "the new classification may force a number of investors in these towns to reconsider and move elsewhere. It may stop the development of these towns following the change of classification. Enterprises are interested in the A classification. If they do not enjoy the terms given to other development regions they will most likely move to Judea and Samaria (the West Bank) in areas near the coast (the primacy region) and thus enjoy all benefits denied to them in the Galilee.[38]

The head of the development towns department in the Ministry of Industry and Trade is also, by title, coordinator of the government of Israel in the Galilee. It appears then that there is a commitment to assure the economic viability of the development towns but that control remains divided within the confederated structure of the Israeli government. An illustrative example is the town of Yeruham. One government commission classified it as an A town, another commission classified it as B (on the list of subsidies).[39] The Ministry of Construction and Housing gives Yeruham an A rating. These classifications are based on each ministry's emphasis. For example, the Ministry of Construction and Housing considers population dispersal as a criterion; the Ministry of Industry and Trade uses instead a broad criterion of advancing settlements with a population of less than 10,000, which is the minimum required for an independently supported unit.

The scope of the chapter does not permit complete discussion of all incentives. Mention should be made, however, of one additional program. The Ministry of Labor and Social Welfare runs a program of directing people to development regions. It advertises the incentives and support it offers, which include rent support, professional allowances, etc., on national television and in the press. In the past five years the Ministry supported the transfer of 2,821 people to development towns.[40]

## Viability of New Towns

Measures of in-and out-migration give a final outcome. Below are some basic data (Table 2.4) for a sample of sixteen development towns and a discussion of factors contributing to the viability of the towns. Obviously, the relative weight of the factors varies; the causes for in- and out-migration can be pinpointed only in a more precise, causal type of analysis. Table 2.4 shows the number of people in sixteen development towns and the year of their establishment, and the various balances of migration. It shows a dynamic process of individual choice. The government, as a matter of policy, is much concerned with the success of the development towns; consequently, it views negative balances of migration with some alarm. However, this pattern of change is a common phenomenon in other countries.

## Table 2.4

## NUMBER OF INHABITANTS AND INTERNAL MIGRATION BALANCE IN SIXTEEN DEVELOPMENT TOWNS

| Town | # of Inhabitants | | # Arriving less # Leaving = Difference | | | | | |
|---|---|---|---|---|---|---|---|---|
| | 1955 | 1982 | 1971-72 | | | 1981-82 | | |
| Or Akiva (1951) | 1,700 | 19,800 | 212 | 271 | (59) | 276 | 466 | (180) |
| Eilat (1951) | 500 | 19,600 | 2869 | 855 | 2014 | 2594 | 2725 | (131) |
| Ofakim (1955) | 600 | 12,700 | 364 | 509 | (137) | 531 | 746 | (215) |
| Beersheba (1948) | 20,500 | 112,600 | 4833 | 3034 | 1799 | 3910 | 4602 | -692 |
| Beit Shean (1948) | 6,400 | 13,500 | 426 | 498 | -71 | 275 | 539 | -264 |
| Beit Shemesh (1950) | 3,000 | 13,000 | 466 | 350 | 166 | 465 | 603 | -138 |
| Dimona (1955) | 300 | 27,600 | 1274 | 1313 | -39 | 729 | 1507 | 527 |
| Hatzor Haglilit (1953) | 2,000 | 6,500 | 84 | 219 | -135 | 281 | 326 | -45 |
| Yeruham (1951) | 500 | 6,600 | 259 | 204 | 55 | 300 | 337 | 53 |
| Migdal Ha'emek (1952) | 2,700 | 14,100 | 837 | 315 | 522 | 427 | 592 | -165 |
| Ma'alot (1957) | 1,300 | 5,200 | 219 | 156 | 63 | 592 | 389 | 203 |
| Netivot (1957) | — | 8,500 | 180 | 159 | 21 | 401 | 343 | 58 |
| Kiryat Gat (1956) | — | 24,900 | 923 | 486 | 437 | 407 | 375 | 32 |
| Kiryat Malachi (1951) | 2,700 | 12,400 | 529 | 608 | -79 | 1005 | ?? | ?? |
| Kiryat Shmona (1960) | — | 15,900 | 382 | 631 | -249 | 624 | ?? | ?? |
| Sederot (1951) | 1,000 | 9,000 | 692 | 583 | 9 | 307 | 348 | -41 |

Sources: The 1955 and 1982 columns are taken from Population in Localities Numbering Above 5,000: Inhabitants on 31.12.82, *Statistical Abstract of Israel*, 1983, Table B/15; Internal Migration Balance in Municipalities and Local Councils, *Local Authorities in Israel 1971/72: Physical Data*, No. 419, Jerusalem 1973, Table 6, pp. 16-17; Internal Migration Between Localities and Settling of Immigration by Local Authority, *Local Authorities in Israel 1981/82: Physical Data*, No. 719, Jerusalem, 1983, Table 9, pp. 45-46.

Table 2.5

PERCENTAGE OF GOVERNMENT PARTICIPATION IN REGULAR BUDGETS
OF DEVELOPMENT TOWNS

| | 1971-72 | | | 1980-81 | | |
|---|---|---|---|---|---|---|
| | % | IL Thousand | | % | IL Thousand | |
| | | Govt | Budget | | Govt | Budget |
| Or Akiva | 58.4 | 1,959 | 2,579 | 83.8 | 12,590 | 15,020 |
| Eilat | 29.6 | 3,448 | 11,684 | 69.1 | 49,167 | 71,098 |
| Ofakim | 66.2 | 3,548 | 5,359 | 89.1 | 28,408 | 31,883 |
| Beersheba | 35.4 | 14,177 | 39,953 | 63.7 | 145,100 | 227,577 |
| Beit Shean | 77.9 | 6,436 | 8,263 | 81.9 | 25,891 | 31,672 |
| Beit Shemesh | 73.1 | 4,193 | 5,740 | 86.3 | 25,830 | 29,940 |
| Dimona | 59.5 | 7,386 | 12,403 | 81.4 | 50,834 | 62,473 |
| Hatzor Haglilit | 29.0 | 2,161 | 2,798 | No data | No data | No data |
| Yeruham | 66.0 | 2,012 | 3,050 | 84.2 | 21,930 | 26,040 |
| Migdal Ha'emek | 67.2 | 3,516 | 5,229 | 83.0 | 28,470 | 34,156 |
| Ma'alot | 78.4 | 2,263 | 2,887 | 86.5 | 16,376 | 18,917 |
| Netivot | 57.7 | 1,998 | 3,470 | 83.8 | 16,820 | 20,078 |
| Kiryat Malachi | 65.4 | 3,059 | 4,671 | 81.1 | 26,633 | 32,833 |
| Kiryat Gat | 45.3 | 5,820 | 12,865 | 76.1 | 51,674 | 67,860 |
| Kiryat Shmona | 64.1 | 4,935 | 7,703 | 83.5 | 34,974 | 41,956 |
| Sederot | 42.0 | 1,472 | 3,510 | 86.3 | 21,469 | 24,874 |

Sources: Central Bureau of Statistics, *Local Authorities in Israel: Financial Data 1971/72. No. 425*, Jerusalem, 1973, Table 10, pp. 32-34, 38-44; *Local Authorities in Israel: Financial Data 1980/81. No. 709*, Jerusalem, 1983, Tables 19, 20, pp. 25-30, 31-36.

Table 2.5 shows the extent of government support for the regular service budget of these communities. On a per capita calculation we find that the central government share in the development towns is up to four times the per capita share in the major cities. Some of these towns can hardly be said to be viable when they are unable to mobilize resources from local sources. However, the important factor for our discussion is the government's policy of support and commitment to these towns. The high share of government support also suggests a potentially high level of interventive capacity. It should be noted, however, that high government support often indicates commitment but not necessarily interventive power. Through politics and links with national parties, for example, a town is likely to receive resources. During 1986-87 the development towns demanded resources — in spite of economic austerity programs — at the expense of the settlements on the West Bank. They found an ally in the Labor party, which opposes the continuous settlement of the West Bank. The government also acts as an equalizer of opportunities. It provides what R. Dye called a minimum service level.[41] A previous study has shown how government intervention is able to improve a town's position as regards per capita expenditure for major services.[42]

## Factors Affecting Individual Choice

The reason why people make a choice to leave a place of residence in metropolitan and rural areas has been the subject of much research.[43] A variety of factors are involved in the decision of a person to move. For example, one might consider the relative weight of the economic situation of the domicile in comparison with the forces of attraction of the target area. An important variable with regard to development towns in Israel is the initial act of population mix by government action. This is likely to be critical to the new town's viability. A. Berler noted the importance of having differential economic levels and differential levels of professional status.[44]

Because concern here is with urban policy, discussion of the major factors that contribute to in-out migration must take into account the following question: Can government policy undermine the negative effect of the elements that contribute to a decision to leave a town? Relative weights of the various factors are not provided here. They are referred to as evidence of what the government must undertake in order to retain viability, avoid abandonment, and actually encourage people to stay in the remoter places.

A study of a development town located near a security border that was the object of shelling from across the border revealed low out-migration, contrary to expectations, in spite of high unemployment.[45] This highlights an important notion: not only are internal town factors to be considered, but the outside economic forces of pull are a key factor. Following security tension (shelling, etc.), there is often increased government support in the form of an input of resources and incentives. However, the additional support rendered by the government often does not affect peoples' decision to leave.[46]

Ethnic origin among those who chose to leave is another contributing factor. The number of people of Western origin who chose to leave is higher than those of the lower socioeconomic strata of Eastern origin. Westerners are generally more able to move because they are likely to have supporting relatives in the primacy areas. Recent revisionist writings claim that a greater number of Jews of Western (European) origin left the more remote settlements for the prime cities much earlier than the Jews of Eastern origin (Arab countries and North Africa). The literature often discusses these issues more as a challenge to alleged discriminatory practices of population absorption rather than as an urban issue.[47]

The very smallness of Israel is another factor in moving out of development towns. As early as 1969, Amiram and Shachar noted the attractiveness of the larger primacy places and how this endangers the government's dispersal policy.[48] This rather common sense type of finding becomes more significant in relation to a recent study that points not to problems such as unemployment, but to the stigma with which some development towns are plagued and the socioeconomic status of the residents.[49] Studies have repeatedly shown that the new towns have many features that do not attract those who freely choose a place to live.

This brief outline of factors contributing to migration can also be taken in reverse (i.e., that improved economic conditions, housing, education, security, ethnic mix, type of employment, etc., can contribute to the retention of population and promote in-migration). The following conclusion can be made: government incentives and economic policy are key factors in contributing to regional and town viability. The effect of government incentive policies on manufacturing spatial distribution, for example, has been researched by Gradus and Krakover.[50]

One can question continued government support for selected towns on economic or urban grounds, but there is little room to question government policy when it reflects generally agreed upon societal goals. The new towns policy is a case in point. In such a case one can deal with outcomes, some of which are unanticipated. For example, some new towns would not have been located where they are, were it not for the government's desire to show Jewish presence in the area. Government policies are likely to reverse the negative effects of factors contributing to the abandonment of towns. In a centrist system such as in Israel, the government controls the level of unemployment, subsidies, and incentives. This was identified in the past history of the new towns. The government can direct industry to the new towns, either by subsidies or by channelling production orders, but the will to do this is primarily political. In terms of national policy there seems to be a continuous government role. The government has to correct what it created by acting against the forces of the market or by complimenting them. In sum, government policy cannot but help contribute to social and economic problems; over time the government obviously has to counteract these problems.

## Proposal for Reforms

A variety of factors led to a clear need for reform and change in the government's attitude and goals, and in the organization of its relations with the development towns. Foremost was the basic reality that emerged in the past thirty years. Some of the towns remain economically highly dependent on central support. Others have passed a take-off stage. Old towns were added to the list of development towns by political pressure in order to become eligible for government support and incentives (e.g., Kfar Tavor and Ramat Ishai and the many settlements in Judea and Samaria).

The renewed commitment of the government (following the 1984 elections) to the development towns took a variety of forms:

1) Mayors of development towns established a forum for negotiation with the government.
2) The political debate over the national settlement effort in the West Bank made salient the relative neglect of the development towns in Israel proper.

3) More recently (1987) key national unity government ministers Ariel Sharon, David Levy, Moshe Katzav and Gad Yacobi competed for the reactivated post of chairman of the Interministerial Government Committee for Development Towns.

4) Prime Minister Peres restated the government's commitment to support new industries in the development towns even at the expense of investment in the West Bank.

5) Economics Minister Yacobi submitted proposed legislation for capital investment and incentives to entrepreneurs in development towns. Minister Katzav surveyed all industries in the towns and proposed ways to foster their capital and technological base, and Deputy Prime Minister Levy outlined a housing expansion program for these towns.

6) Stringent efforts were made by Minister of Labor and Social Welfare Moshe Katzav, who is himself a former mayor of a development town, to place the issue on the public agenda, which resulted in the establishment of a commission whose task it was to outline the major lines of national government policy regarding the new towns.[51] The major proposals of the commission include a new classification of settlements entitled to be called development towns and hence eligible for various incentives.

The new classification is based on distance from the center, and on economic and social viability. Based on these criteria, 21 development towns emerged and 13 old towns were removed from the list.[52] An additional proposal argues for a separate, transitional, two-level incentive system: 11 additional towns would be high incentive towns and 10 towns low incentive ones.[53] Urban settlements would be eligible for inclusion in the development town category. The community category, with a population of higher economic potential, would be subsidized only in land purchase and personal loans. Another major proposal by the commission relates to policy coordination and control. The commission proposed the reestablishment of the dormant Government Interministerial Committee for Development Towns. Up to the present time development towns policy was handled by a government Committee of Welfare, which did not deal exclusively with development towns. The importance of the new development town policy is attested to by four separate government ministerial proposals for classification of what is a development town and what incentives should be made available.

47

Had the settlement pattern in the areas of the West Bank and the Gaza Strip since the ascent of the Likud Party to power in 1977 been undertaken in less inhospitable international political conditions, the thrust of the effort would have been considered exemplary national planning policy and control. It is probable that only under high pressure can policies (which include not only settlements but also major regional cities) of this scope be undertaken. The settlement pattern was initially influenced by national security considerations as defined by successive Israeli governments. The Jordan River is viewed as Israel's eastern security line. It is a natural barrier. The area of the West Bank has about 800,000 Arab inhabitants. The Palestinians view it as an area where the state they aspire to might emerge; Jordan and Israel are in dispute over the area. The relative status quo and growing Arab threats dictate old and familiar conceptions: one acquires legitimacy over disputed territory by establishing a physical presence in the form of settlements, especially where projected future borders are likely to be negotiated.

Up to 1972, the ruling Labor party asserted a historic right to the West Bank but argued that settlements were to reflect security conceptions as outlined in the Allon plan.[54] When the Likud came to power in 1977, they took the security considerations for granted and underlined the ideological element. A look at the settlement map of Labor shows a preponderance of settlements along the Jordan River, but few within the West Bank proper. The Likud's map is more dispersed throughout. It reflects more strongly an ideology of control and presence, and historic rights. A clearly identifiable Likud government policy directed massive resources to the development of infrastructure and settlements in the West Bank. The Ministry of Defense was a major decision-maker in the planning policy and implementation process, and this assured a high level of control and execution. The settlers in the West Bank area are mostly ideologists of a greater Israel. This only facilitated government policy. The willing settlers were a far cry from the reluctant newcomers to Israel's development towns.

Settlement patterns in the West Bank are also influenced by Gush Emunim, a highly effective political pressure group, and more recently by a new political party, Tehiya, which up to the 1984 elections controlled the government's settlement committee. When government action was viewed as too slow, Gush Emunim simply occupied open public land or purchased land from Arabs and staked a claim. The government allowed itself to follow where it feared to lead. One famous case was Sebastia, near the major Arab city of Nablus, where between 1974 and 1976 the Labor government gave in to pressure and allowed a settlement that transcended security considerations. Later, during the Likud government, the city of Ariel was expanded. There emerged around it lesser cities, rural towns, and a privately sponsored and financed city.

Israel's settlement effort has increased the urban industrial base in the Gaza area and the West Bank, which were previously mostly rural regions. Table 2.6 details the number of settlements Israel established in the area. There is much debate about the number of Israelis who actually settled in the territories. Figures vary from 30,000 to 70,000 people.

Table 2.6

SETTLEMENTS IN THE TERRITORIES, 1974-83

|  | Number of Settlements by Type | |
|  | Urban | Rural |
| --- | --- | --- |
| Judea and Samaria | 5 | 113 |
| Gaza | – | 10 |
| Golan | 1 | 29 |

Source: E. Efrat, *Geography and Politics in Israel* (Tel Aviv: Ahiasaf 1983), pp. 91-95, 123, 134, 153 (Hebrew).

## Land Regulation and Population Movement

A concrete element of rural ideology found its way into the first amendment to the 1965 Planning and Housing Law (PHL) via the Committee for the Preservation of Agricultural Land (CPAL). The CPAL regulates the activities of urban planning institutions and plans conformity as far as agriculturally designated lands are concerned. Through its veto and benefit allocation powers, it also determines the scope of land development.

Its regulative role is outlined in article 49 of the Law.[55] Item I prescribes that agricultural lands be preserved and the CPAL oversee national, regional and local plans regarding their compliance with the preservation of land fit for agriculture (the committee also has regulative power over forests and open spaces). Although its administrative structure is meager, the CPAL exerts a dominant influence on urban policy through piecemeal, allocative intervention during the various planning stages. The CPAL has the statutory power to declare land as agricultural land. Up to the present time, the members of the committee have by and large represented the agricultural sector and almost by definition have been sensitive to agricultural interest groups. The CPAL is faced with constant appeals by cities and towns to change land designation and thus enable urban growth. A forthcoming study of the CPAL found that it is able to block or expand urban development by rulings regarding the appropriateness of land for agriculture. The CPAL's role is dealt with in full in chapter 4.

The government in Israel has a key role in urban development. It is estimated that some 90 percent of the land is owned by the government. When the government stands neutral vis-a-vis decisions, urban development of agriculturally designated land cannot take place. The CPAL can also influence development in towns and rural settlements. The scarcity with which agricultural lands are released for use for housing or development determines the cost of housing and people's life style. The more land that is released, the faster urban revitalization can take place in deteriorating towns and in decaying areas. In semi-urban towns it is often difficult to find the proper balance between conflicting urban and rural needs. The policy of restricting land use is government policy, albeit influenced by the previously dominant rural interests, but it is debatable whether this is the proper policy for urban growth.

The policy of preserving agricultural land emerged as one of the outcomes of the previously dominant ruralism. But it also stands in line with other policies such as population dispersal and open land policy. It is unlikely that in the original initiation of the policy of the preservation of agricultural land, the current metropolitan growth in the major urban areas was foreseen. Despite this misgiving, the CPAL does perform a useful function in eliminating the speculative value of agricultural land. Through the CPAL, agricultural land in urban centers becomes open space. For example, the city of Tel Aviv has about 800 acres of agricultural land, and its adjacent suburb, Ramat Hasharon, some 3,000 acres. The population density expected for the year 1992 in the region is 1,376 persons per acre; according to the city's master plan, the population of Tel Aviv is expected to be about 460,000 compared with 320,000 today. The agricultural lands will not, of course, provide the space for such growth.

## Controlled Increase of Population

The government makes deliberate efforts to increase the share of the Jewish population in some cities and in those regions of Israel that have a large non-Jewish population. This policy is referred to in the vernacular as *Yehud*, which means Judaization. The policy is accompanied by special administrative structures and resource allocations. Cases in point are the northern region of the Galilee and Jerusalem. The West Bank area may be included, although there one can speak in terms of settlement and urban policy.

Uneven regional development has been the object of much research in many political systems; it has also become a recognized academic specialization. Attempts have been made to characterize Israel in terms of regional-territorial political behavior.[56] It is open to debate, however, whether Israel possesses features of regionalism, given its 4,500,000 people and a travel distance from north to south of 537 kilometers. A condition for the identification of a regional will is the emergence of regional interest. This is hardly likely given the fact that, for example, many of the rural settlements in the Galilee region are affiliated with national organizations. The kibbutzim and moshavim settlements in the Galilee would be very hesitant to depart from their powerful national associations, which are affiliated with the Labor movement. This political aspect was overlooked by Gradus when he more than hinted at the emergence of regional interest.[57]

Israeli regional governmental policies are better discussed in terms of their effective and coordinated field administration.[58] Regional interests are channelled through the national organizations, which in turn deal with the central government. From the central government perspective, a greater and more coherent national urban policy and service delivery systems in the regions would be achieved through tighter coordination of the implementation agencies. However, this is difficult to come by given the politically confederated structure of governmental agencies. The fact that the regions operate under a long managerial tradition of direct relations between single settlements and central agencies, and only to a lesser degree with governmental field offices, hinders the introduction of concerted government action. Any discussion of regionalism must also take into account decentralization and area participation. The current situation is that the central government oversees urban and other development. For example, the current government's role can be seen in the specific programs to increase the Jewish population in the Galilee. Central plans resulted in the establishment of the network of 28 mini-settlements, which are actually housing neighborhoods located in strategic locations to demonstrate Jewish presence and potential.

An example of deliberate urban development is Jerusalem. After the Six Day War in 1967, Israel gained control over the entire city and its vicinity. Between 1967 and 1984 the population of the city doubled. The reclamation and rebuilding of the Jewish Quarter in the Old City, and the construction of six new Jewish neighborhoods around the city, was jointly undertaken and executed by the city, under the leadership of Mayor Kollek, and the Israeli government through the Ministry of Housing. This deliberate urban policy was executed at great speed, and a huge amount of central resources were applied. It exposed what I call a parallel process of planning which brought with it severe conflict. Government commitment to the increased growth of Jerusalem was such that the city planners and administration became dedicated to the task of returning planning to the city.[59] Their commitment came into conflict with the relevant government ministry regarding the potential negative aesthetic results to the city from the forceful government development and construction thrust. This issue highlighted the interorganizational network of planning policy. Prime Minister Golda Meir often took on the role of arbitrator between the various actors involved in order to achieve quick settlements. She emulated the early precedent of Ben-Gurion's direct involvement in the new towns and dispersal policies.

## Neighborhood Renewal

The Neighborhood Renewal and Rehabilitation Project policy (Project Renewal) was initiated following the ascent to power of the Likud center-right party in June 1977. The projects under this policy were aimed to assist populations in distressed neighborhoods. The government intended a new approach to community renewal that would include social and community rehabilitation through citizen participation. To give the policy the broadest possible commitment it was decided that the project would be a joint undertaking of the Israeli government and world Jewry.

Project Renewal meets the criteria set out here of a national urban policy. Its various programs are accompanied by political commitment, an elaborate administrative structure, procedures of resource allocation, and controls that include identifiable self-correcting mechanisms. Project Renewal has an inter-organizational decision structure and a degree of institutionalized citizen participation.

Project Renewal superseded slum clearance programs that were previously carried out by the Ministry of Construction and Housing under a specially designated 1965 law that limited the programs to clearance and redevelopment, but with hardly any provision for physical improvements. While in 1972, $2 million was budgeted for eight neighborhoods, in 1977, at the beginning of Project Renewal, nearly $14 million was allocated to about fifteen neighborhoods.[60]

The government of Israel provided administrative instruments for the implementation of Project Renewal by establishing an interministerial committee headed by the deputy prime minister. In order to give emphasis to the individual and community rehabilitation features of the program, the committee was named the Social and Welfare Ministerial Committee. A national policy steering committee outlined strategies of implementation, and the partnership with world Jewry added to the formalization of the renewal policy. The result was a formal control system with mutual prodding for action. By 1979, 25 neighborhoods were included, 39 were added in 1980, and by 1982 there were 80 neighborhoods.

## Resources and Control

By 1984, the cumulative allocation for Project Renewal was about $400 million, of which the government of Israel provided $250 million and world Jewry $150 million.[61] The year-by-year increase since 1978 reflects the incorporation of new neighborhoods and the extension of the scope of the programs. Early activities focused on physical improvement in living conditions; later, neighborhood environment programs such as parks and gardens were implemented, and more recently much emphasis was placed on social development programs that include enrichment and head-start activities.

The residents themselves take part in the planning of the social programs through decision forums that give the locale a large measure of control over the type of programs to be instituted. A study of one of the neighborhoods in Tel Aviv revealed that the residents defined their needs in terms of education.[62] Local government officials and the administrators of Project Renewal agreed that the program was more than just an urban renewal undertaking. Consequently, resources were applied toward a variety of educational, psychological and enrichment programs for adults and children. Control of these activities was twofold: (1) the actors (residents) and the actual activities became a part of the bureaucratic implementation process, and (2) the residents became persistent defenders of the programs. This type of control is not possible in a standard hierarchical arrangement. In the case of Project Renewal, both the national and local structures of the program had a share in influencing decisions. One advantage of such a complex structure is that it creates a mutual watchdog system. It is, in other words, a tool to control the implementation process.

The desired emphasis on people, social features and the community was, at first, unsuccessful. Emphasis was placed on physical housing and environmental renewal. This occurred for a number of reasons. Project Renewal had raised high expectations. It was necessary to begin with projects that produced immediate results. The complex organizational structure was such that quick feedback was necessary in order to mobilize further resources. Jewish communities from countries around the world required concrete evidence when they visited their adopted towns and neighborhoods. Physical renewal gave the whole policy, including the social community aspects, its necessary momentum. There were additional reasons for the early emphasis on the physical features. Bad housing conditions were the catalyst for local steering committees. They supported the early emphasis on reconstructions. Once this was achieved there occurred a shift in emphasis to the social and educational aspects of the programs. Within the context of the rehabilitation of deteriorating neighborhoods in the cities and in previously established new towns, Project Renewal involves many of the policy elements outlined earlier. It can be said to reflect a national urban policy.

## Concluding Summary

Various policy elements were outlined at the beginning of this chapter. The policy elements were viewed as essential determinants of a national urban policy and were used to gauge the specific discussion of national urban policy in Israel. It was pointed out that these elements are universal and can be applied comparatively to systems other than Israel.

### Political Commitment

New towns and dispersal policies require a political commitment, which was evident in the high consensus among the ruling elite regarding these policies. Conflict over the new towns policy was generated by the planners of the rural section. New towns development represented a planning concept of a hierarchical, spatial distribution of settlements that would negate the former polar model, which had historical roots and did not provide for intermediate size towns in the hinterland. The hierarchical planning conception was an innovation that required new political support, notwithstanding the inclination of the social labor elite toward the rural development features of the polar modes. Political support was forthcoming in the context of new national goals that arose after the establishment of the state. The pattern was repeated in the West Bank, where political commitment followed the acquisition of territory and was then strengthened by the ideology of the ruling groups. The political commitment to the new towns policy, the non-polar planning concept, and settlement of the West Bank, had a variety of rewards for the ruling parties. It contributed to Israel's presence and control of relatively vast areas, and the policies helped popularize the issues as national goals.

### Ordered Planning and Implementation

With the adoption of the new hierarchical planning approach, urban policy became a formalized viable domain. Indeed, the actual establishment of towns was an ordered process in concept and administration. It penetrated the ideologized milieu of agrarianism and operated in parallel and interactively with the huge rural

55

planning sector and its aims. For example, the Lachish region settlement plan launched by Prime Minister Ben-Gurion was an instance where professional planning gave procedural expression to normative features involving control of territory and nation-building. The element of planning and ordered implementation was also a salient factor in the national policies in the West Bank and in the policy of neighborhood renewal. In both domains there was an overt political commitment that aided the ordered implementation. It appears that ruling groups that have the capacity to initiate national urban policies and generate the framework for implementation strategy are likely to reap varied political benefits.

## Identifiable Procedures of Control

The very deliberateness with which the implementation of urban policy strategies were followed suggests a certain level of control. The elaborate administrative structure surrounding the effort assured a variety of correction mechanisms. Control was aided by political commitment, administration, planning, and the continuity of projects. Other contributing factors were that the success of the development towns was a major national concern. Not surprisingly, new towns drew resources in their direction. Research and evaluation accompanied the process. For example, the ideal ethnic combination of a new town constantly occupied the attention of implementers and researchers. The ongoing evaluation of the new towns policy resulted in a variety of correcting programs, which involved housing for the young and the moving of public institutions to new towns. Control was facilitated by the institutionalization of procedures concerning the allocation of national resources, which included a well-defined system of incentives and subsidies. This was also the case in the planning of Jerusalem.

Control over the overall governmental commitment to a policy such as new towns does not, of course, assure success in specific instances. The strong governmental interventive role was often mitigated by a free market, which modified the government's ability to control the policy. High government commitment often meant control over resource allocation to failing enterprises. The continuity of government support to failing towns, for example, required a new support policy that was an outcome of the original commitment to the new towns policy. Lastly, it should be noted that the Israeli commitment to the new towns policy often negated the ability to truly intervene and correct. A town's leader could rely on the national commitment and urge only a minimum of local effort.

## Ordered Allocations: Incentives and Subsidies

National direction of urban policy is facilitated through incentives and subsidies. It can take a variety of forms. In the West Bank, for example, the government provides infrastructure financing in the context of direct incentives and subsidies to individuals and firms. The pattern is not new; it was used in the implementation of urban policy in new towns in Israel proper. A variety of government corporations provide subsidies, tax incentives and grants to investors. New towns receive different classifications relating to the subsidies and incentives to which they are entitled.

In summary, to achieve a high level of control of a national urban policy, one would expect intensive coordination effects to be apparent. This is difficult to introduce given systemic features such as the interorganizational decision networks that exist in Israel. Notwithstanding this difficulty, national urban policy in Israel shows identifiable administrative features that could be the focus of further research. For example, the level of coordination and control is not the same for all programs and all agencies. In the initiation stage there is great saliency to the policies, at which time there are likely to be more coherent activities than in later stages when correction mechanisms are set in motion. Hierarchical coordinators and controls are not likely to be found over time in a system such as Israel's with its federation of government ministries and coalition government.

## Notes — Chapter 2

1. Blair, John P. and Nachmias, David. *Fiscal Retrenchment and Urban Policy*. Beverly Hills: Sage Publications, 1979.
2. Doig, Jameson W. and Danielson, Michael N. "The Role of Government in Urban Development," *Policy Studies Journal* 8 (Summer 1980):852-861.
3. Kasarada, John D. "The Implications of Contemporary Redistribution Trends for National Urban Policy," *Social Science Quarterly* 6 (December 1980):373-400.
4. Richardson, Harry W. "National Urban Development Strategies in Developing Countries," *Urban Studies* 18 (1981):270.
5. Landau, Martin. "Redundancy, Rationality and the Problem of Duplication and Overlap," *Public Administration Review* 20 (1969):346-358.
6. Gurewitz, David and Geretz, Aharon. *The Jewish Yishuv in Eretz Israel*. Jerusalem: Statistics Department, Jewish Agency, Bulletin 21, 1940.
7. Schachar, Arie, *et al. Cities in Israel*. Jerusalem: Academon, 1973, pp. 41-42, 70-119 (Hebrew).
8. Brutzkus, Eliezer. "Planning of Population Dispersal," *Rivon Lekalkala* 1 (May, 1964):39-55 (Hebrew); see also Richardson, Harry W., "Polarization Reversal in Developing Countries," *Papers of the Regional Science Association* 45 (1980):67-85.
9. Resolution of the 13th Zionist Congress in Carlsbad. London: Zionist Federation Report, 1923.
10. *Ibid.* See also Rupin, Arthur. *The Agricultural Settlements of the Zionist Federation in Eretz Israel*. Tel Aviv: Dvir Publication, 1925 (Hebrew).
11. *Ibid.*
12. Gorni, Joseph. *Achdut Haavoda 1919-1930: Ideological Foundation and Political Method*. Tel Aviv: Kibbutz Hameuchad, 1973 (Hebrew).
13. Shapira, Jonathan. *The Power of Political Organizations: Achdut Haavoda in Historical Perspective*. Tel Aviv: Am Oved, 1975 (Hebrew); Giladi, Dan. *The Yishuv During the Fourth Aliya 1924-1929*. Jerusalem: Hebrew University, 1968 (Hebrew).
14. Cohen, Eric. *The City in Zionist Ideology*. Jerusalem: Hebrew University, 1972 (Hebrew).
15. Slosky, Yehuda. Introduction to the *History of the Labor Movement*. Tel Aviv: Am Oved, 1973 (Hebrew); Tartakover, Arie. "City and Village in Eretz Israel," *Kama, Yearbook of the Jewish National Fund, 1968*, pp. 121-136 (Hebrew).

16. Borochov, Ben. *Selected Writings*. Tel Aviv: Am Oved, 1944, esp. pp. 210-211 (Hebrew).
17. Shechter, Asaf. *The Works of A.D. Gordon*. Tel Aviv: Dvir Publications, 1957 (Hebrew).
18. Shapira, *The Power of Political Organizations*.
19. Giladi, *The Yishuv During the Fourth Aliya*, pp. 36-40, 176.
20. Data based on regional division. See Sikron, Moshe and Lesman, Benjamin, "Changes in the Population of the Regions 1961-1972," *City and Region* 3 (January 1976):3-25.
21. *Haaretz*, (25 September 1984).
22. Torgovnik, Efraim. "A Perspective on Central Metropolitan Relations," *Journal of Comparative Administration* 3 (February 1972):469-490.
23. Kubersky, Haim. *Commission for National Allocations*. Jerusalem: Ministry of Interior; National Commission for Local Affairs, *Local Government in Israel* (The Sanbar Commission) (Jerusalem, 1981); National Commission for Reform in the Dan Area, *Reports*, Vol. 1-6 (Jerusalem, 1971).
24. Torgovnik, Efraim and Barzel, Yeshayahu. *Statistical Abstract of Israel*, No. 2, 1950/51.
25. Cohen, *The City in Zionist Ideology*, p. 1; Borochov, *Selected Writings*, p. 210.
26. Ministry of Interior, *National Plans for Population Dispersal*. Jerusalem: Ministry of Interior, National Planning Council; Brutzkus, Eliezer. "Plans for Geographic Distribution of the Population in Israel of Five Million," in *City and Region* 1 (April 1933):3-25 (Hebrew); Gal, Sharon. "Social Aspect in the Geographic Distribution of Israel," *Environmental Planning* 26 (December 1979):19-30; Sikron and Lesman, "Changes in the Population of the Regions, 1961-1972."
27. Sikron and Lesman, "Changes in the Population of the Regions, 1961-1972," p. 7.
28. Reichman, Shalom. "On the Validity of the Plans for Geographic Distribution of the Population of Israel," *City and Region* 3 (April 1973):26-43 (Hebrew).
29. Soen, Dan. "Migration Balance and Socio-Economic Image — The Case of Israel's New Towns," *Planning Outlook* 26 (1983):22-27 (Hebrew).
30. Shachar *et al.*, *Cities in Israel*; Reichman, "On the Validity of the Plans for Geographic Distribution," pp. 26-43.
31. Aronoff, Michael. *Frontier Towns. The Politics of Community Building in Israel*. Manchester: Manchester University Press, 1974.

32. Berler, Alexander. *New Towns in Israel*. Jerusalem: University Press in Israel, 1970; Lichfield, Nathaniel. *Israel's New Towns: A Development Strategy*, vols. 1-3. Jerusalem: Ministry of Housing, 1971 (Hebrew); Spiegel, Erika. *New Towns in Israel*. New York: Praeger Press, 1967; Efrat, Elisha. *Cities and Urbanization in Israel*. Tel Aviv: Ahiasaf, 1976 (Hebrew).
33. *Ibid.*
34. Borochov, Eli and Werczberger, Elia. "Factors Affecting the Development of New Towns in Israel." Tel Aviv: The Pinhas Sapir Center for Development, Tel Aviv University Paper No. 2-80, February 1980 (Hebrew).
35. For more information on the growth of political leadership see Torgovnik, Efraim and Weiss, Shevah. "Local Non-Party Political Organization," *Western Political Quarterly* 25 (1972).
36. "Ministry of Housing Offer of Loans for Housing Settlement" (June 1984), Jerusalem: Ministry of Housing (Hebrew); "List of Incentives to People Who Settle in Development Towns," Ministry of Labor and Social Welfare, Center for Diversion to Development Towns (15 July 1984) (Hebrew).
37. The Law for the Encouragement of Investments, 1959.
38. Green, David. *Lisafim* 194 (12 March 1984):4-5 (Hebrew).
39. Kochav, David. *Report of Interministerial Committee for Dispersal Policy*. Jerusalem, 1969 (Hebrew); Naor, Gideon. *Report on Development Town Classification*. Jerusalem: Interministerial Committee on Classification, 1972.
40. Naor, *ibid.*; Naor, Gideon. "Recommendation of Expert Report on Classification of Development Towns," *Environmental Planning* (1972).
41. Dye, James. *Understanding Public Policy*. Englewood Cliffs, N.J.: Prentice-Hall, 1978.
42. Torgovnik, Efraim. "Central Aid and Local Policy," *Public Finance Quarterly* 6 (April 1978):211-239.
43. Kirschenbaum, Alan. *Selective Migration and Population Redistribution: A Study of New Towns in Israel*. Haifa: Technion, 1972; Hansen, H.E. *Location Preferences, Migration and Regional Growth*. New York: Praeger, 1973.
44. Cohen, Eric. "Problems of Development Towns and Urban Neighborhoods," *Economic Quarterly* 13 (June 1966):117-131 (Hebrew); Berler, Alexander. *Absorption in New Towns and Rural Hinterland*. Rehovot: Settlement Research Center, 1970; Berber, *New Towns in Israel*.
45. Zuckerman-Bareli, Haya. "Factors in Leaving Development Towns," *Economic Quarterly* 98 (September 1978):192 (Hebrew).
46. *Ibid.*

47. Segev, Tom. *1949, The First Israelis.* Tel Aviv: Domino, 1984 (Hebrew); Svirsky, Shlomo. *Orientals and Ashkenazim in Israel.* Haifa: Papers of Research and Criticism, 1981 (Hebrew).
48. Amiran, David and Shachar, Arie. *Development Towns in Israel.* Jerusalem: The Hebrew University, 1969 (Hebrew).
49. Cohen, "Problems of Development Towns and Urban Neighborhoods," pp. 123-134.
50. Gradus, Yehuda and Eviny, Yaakov. "Trends in Core-Peripheral Industrialization Gaps in Israel," *Geographical Research Forum* 3 (May 1981):25-37 (Hebrew); Gradus, Yehuda and Krakover, S. "The Effort of Government Policy on the Spatial Structure of Manufacturing in Israel," *Journal of Developing Areas* 11 (April 1977):393-409 (Hebrew).
51. Ministry of Labor and Social Welfare, Center for the Direction of People to Development Towns. *Proposal of the Center for Government Policy in Development Towns* (Jerusalem: October 1985).
52. *Ibid.,* pp. 18-19.
53. *Ibid.,* p. 21.
54. The Allon plan is named after a former Labor leader. The plan outlines security zones along the Jordan river and east-west security corridors through the West Bank.
55. Planning and Housing Law, Jerusalem: Ministry of Interior, 1965.
56. Elazar, Daniel J. *Israel—From an Ideological Democracy to a Territorial Democracy.* Ramat Gan: Bar-Ilan University, 1974 (Hebrew).
57. Gradus, Yehuda. "The Role of Politics in Regional Inequality: The Israeli Case," *Annals of Association of American Geographers* 73 (1983):388-403.
58. Partial efforts in this direction have been undertaken by Menuchin, N. and Ludmor, H. *The Second Layer Government in Israel: The Regional Government.* Rehovot: Settlement Research Center, 1982 (Hebrew); and by Brutzkus, E. *Regional Government in Israel* (Jerusalem).
59. Interview with Mayor T. Kollek and City Planner M. Benvenisti.
60. Alexander, A.I. *Neighborhood Clearance in Israel: Administrative and Institutional Aspects.* Haifa: Neaman Institute, 1980 (Hebrew).
61. International Committee for the Evaluation of Project Renewal Neighborhoods. *Report for 1983.* Ministry of Housing and Jewish Agency, February 1984 (Hebrew).
62. Dagani, Avi, *et al. Hatikvah Neighborhood: Methodological Framework.* Tel Aviv: Tel Aviv University, Geography Department, 1979 (Hebrew).

# Chapter 3

# STRUCTURAL DETERMINANTS
# OF PLANNING POLICY

The structural features of an urban planning policy system and the inter-relations therein serve as a basis for an explanation of the nature of planning politics. A set of planning policy strategies might be made in one structure, but not in another. We focus on the structures related to the planning policy process, which can activate individuals and groups that seek access to decision-making. It is important to analyze structures in order to delineate those actors who have direct access to planning policy decisions and who can exclude others, and those who are excluded by systemic structural features. These features of Israeli planning policy underscore a dynamic process and the scope of political accommodations. According to Hanf and Scharpf, structures can facilitate or impede the employment of specific influence strategies.[1] Structures are related to systemic normative features, which find expression in managerial concepts of hierarchy and control. These preferences indicate that those in control of the system have opted for an exclusionary situation. Thus, it is unlikely for strong public participation in planning policy to take place; hierarchy and control are preferred. The politics of planning policy resolve the many conflicts which are generated by these systemic features.

## Local and National Policy Structures

From the late 1960s until the mid 1970s, during an expansionist period, the role of the central government was strengthened vis-a-vis local government in Western systems and in Israel. As the central authority had resources to distribute to the local systems, a change took place in the structure of managerial control and the strings attached (e.g., matching funds, standards of highway construction, comprehensive planning, methods of transportation, etc.). In the late 1970s and early 1980s, a less affluent period, dependence on central authorities increased. In

63

both periods, planning emerged as an important and widespread activity. In the first period planning was used to rationalize the use of resources; later, it was used to maximize the productivity of scarce resources. Professionalism in planning was a by-product of these trends, and its theoretical foundation was the Procedural Planning Theory (see chapter 1).

Politics became a stronger factor in local systems in the 1970s, when competition over resources became fierce. Local politicians challenged the role of the state, and the national and local planning professionals, by claiming to represent the public interest. The growing need for greater coordination of the new and varied demands, actors and organizations involved in planning policy generated change. Old structures and practices had to give way to more accessibility and more coordination. There was also a need to regulate the ability of diverse organizations to obstruct planning policy. Lines of demarcation between goal setting and implementation were needed. The answer was to introduce forums for conflict resolution over policy, which would formalize the role of all interested parties including the planners. Much of this was accomplished in the constitutional and legal reform of the urban planning system in 1965.

The 1965 Planning and Building Law (PBL) formalized the structure of planning and the roles of designated individuals and organizations, and determined the scope of activity in substantive planning domains involving: (1) a hierarchical control system of planning and (2) a Committee for the Preservation of Agricultural land (CPAL). (The land policies of the CPAL and its role as a veto organization are discussed in full in chapter 4). The planning organization structure represents a managerial-political approach to planning; the CPAL represents historical normative ruralism and regulation. The different levels of planning organization set up were a local planning and building commission (LPBC), a regional planning and building commission (RPBC), and a national planning and building council (NPBC). Each level gave access and a decision role to various actors, groups, organizations and planners. Despite being a setting for conflict and confrontation between individuals, organizations and ideologies, this hierarchical structure was also expected to provide coordination. Dominance in planning policy is an empirical question. It cannot be arbitrarily assigned. It is likely to be related to political competition. Research focuses on the roles and influence of individuals, councilmen, groups and organizations which compete within the planning policy decision structures.

## The Role of Ideology

Ideologies have a substantive effect on planning. An ideology is often a self-fulfilling conclusion. An ideology of development, for example, presupposes facts that point to the need for development. Ideologies affect the general orientation of planning policy systems because they touch on the framework of beliefs, viewpoints, values and rationalizations that accompany state and human activity. Ideologies also affect the legal and statutory system through the push and pull of competing values.[2]

McAuslan identified the competing ideologies of laymen, lawyers, politicians and planners. In addition to structural and behavioral features, he also pointed to normative factors. For example, if a system is committed to a pluralistic structure of decision making, we must follow the modes of conflict resolution in order to understand what planning succeeded in accomplishing. Thus, the research emphasis on implementation cannot be considered complete without relating implementation to normative features, to structures, and to politics. Research emphasizes the political elements involved in implementation. Studies that view implementation simply as a head count of what was adopted overlook a great deal of data that could be discovered if the emphasis was political.[3]

Ideology and structure are also important in neo-Marxist writings on planning policy, which view planning as essentially related to the maintenance of the economic and social structure. Under this view, planning professionalism becomes secondary.[4] Substance matters more than procedure. Procedure serves the substance, which is decided by conservative forces who are skillful actors in a given coalition. Israel's planning structures reflect a concern with managerial, state control. This has its roots in the early years of nation building and conquest of land, when the ruling Laborites' planning ideology favored the rural sectors and emphasis was placed on development, population dispersal, and, of course, control. Social investments benefitted collective settlement movements, such as the kibbutzim (collective farms).

We explicate how planning policy is made and how it

functions, given particular structural and normative features. We do not deal with implications regarding social-economic forces, which are legitimized, protected, or enhanced. Since political parties are involved in making planning policy, it is as representative of the various publics as any other policy domain which emerges in a unitary system such as Israel.

## Conflict and Planning Organizations

The 1965 PBL reflects the political factor that divides domains among actors and assures a channel of influence for the many different interests and organizations involved in planning. The structure of the local, regional and national planning organizations reveals the potential conflicts over policy, because each participant is given a role which he may choose to use or ignore. Decisions on planning policy involve interaction among participants, each of whom has different abilities to use political resources. Thus, the structural setting for planning policy is amenable to conflict. An intricate network of relationships is observable; decisions evolve from interaction among a variety of processes and interconnected links.

Blowers views agreement and coalition as being conditions which prevent conflict; in the absence of agreement there will be conflict over policy.[5] We, on the other hand, see conflict as being built into the structure and process of planning. Thus, what Blowers sees as an absence of conflict is actually due to identifiable modes of conflict resolution. The concept of policy consensus used by Blowers could mean that obstacles were removed, that accommodations were made, or that a predominance of actors with political resources generated accommodation. However, it is preferable to view conflict or non-conflict as being the result of political processes that either do or do not achieve conflict resolution and accommodation. Non-agreement and conflict over time is itself a political policy outcome. The intensity of a policy issue, the relative stakes of actors, and the extent to which persisting confrontation serves actors with political resources, determine the outcome. Agreement or disagreement, then, are political-policy decisions.

The local, regional, and national planning and building commissions are hierarchical structures, and so are the plans (see Figure 3.1).[6] For example, a regional plan takes precedence over a local plan; local plans have to conform to regional plans;

both are legally binding. In practice, regional plans take so long to prepare that local plans dominate the scene. Nevertheless, the enactment of plans of an elected local commission requires the approval of the regional commission; only then do the plans become legally binding. This role of the RPBC generates an information flow between the local and regional levels, appeals for exceptions and remedial action, plus bargaining and alliance-building, which in turn determine the political involvement of developers and other actors in the planning process. The local level initiates plans and brings them before the regional level. Local power lies mainly in its domination of the building permit administration. The regional level's strong role in local planning is based on its power to review, delay, correct, approve or reject. It is argued here that there is a lack of congruence between the formal structural hierarchy and the actual behavior concerning the hierarchy of plans.

Figure 3.1

STRUCTURE AND MEMBERSHIP OF
PLANNING ORGANIZATIONS

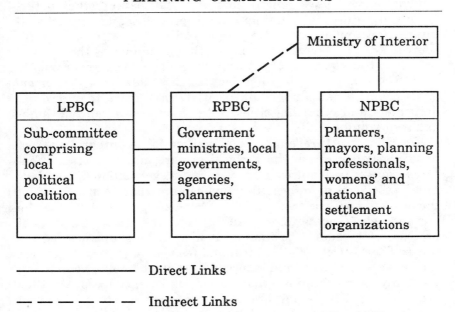

67

When a government ministry acts as a developer, it submits its plans to the local planning commission; the latter passes the plan to the regional planning commission, where the ministry is likely to have a direct voice in the eventual decision. When the city itself is the developer, it is represented on the local commission; professional and political levels seek alliances on the regional commission. When a private developer initiates a project, on both the local and regional planning commissions, he seeks to influence the decision structure.

In this political arena of conflict over planning policy, those who initiate a project know they must work to translate their proposals into policies. In the framework of the planning organizations, the actors use resources to turn a preference into an authoritative course of action: a policy. Of those who hold potential decision roles in a planning organization, some may choose not to be involved in planning-policy issues. In the early stages of initiation and formulation of planning policy, actors are likely to assess whether an issue is worth their activating resources and entering the confrontation. They may choose to remain passive. We should, therefore, be able to distinguish between situations that make an issue active and those that do not.

The following systemic factors are vital, because they determine the nature of planning: (1) the prevalence of conflict and interaction among competing organizations; (2) the use of resources; (3) the constant search for alliances; and (4) the roles of actors in the planning organizations. As few local governments have well organized planning departments, this leaves other organizations in an important position in regard to planning. Jerusalem and other big cities, with their well-organized, high-quality planning units, are exceptions.

In this structure and arena, politics is an integral part of planning policy. From the theoretical perspective, systemic features have to be empirically and comparatively studied. No planning theory can be universally applicable without clarification of the various systemic features. The PPT distinguishes between the environment (substantive position) and the understanding of processes (procedural position), but it must be supplemented because of the variety of structural and normative systemic features that have substantive and (especially) conflict implications.

Analysis of planning organizations is essential because they are where policy issues are activated, where actors of varied stakes, commitments and resources, interact. An organization serves as the basis for involvement in and evolvement of planning policy, and its structure indicates the potential roles of planners in determining policy.

Decisions on land use are made in the planning organizations; land is designated, allocated, and licensed for various uses. Planning organizations are characterized through their position on the general planning hierarchy, and by the degree of control they exercise. The 1965 PBL was intended to create a rational, controlled, goal-oriented system throughout the country. Even though Israel's unitary political system formally allotted power over planning policy to professional planners, giving them a formal role at the regional level and plan preparation roles at all levels, the intention was not realized due to a number of reasons: (1) membership of planning organizations is political. At all three levels of planning, members represent both central and local government; at the local level, members reflect the local political coalition; (2) the political culture of Israel does not encourage professionalism nor policy effectiveness, rather it is concerned with access to and accommodation of the different political forces in society. Effectiveness can be measured on the basis of the goals achieved in the process of conflict resolution. There is no incentive for effectiveness in the 1985 PBL. The RPBC could routinize and rationalize planning by imposing a framework of outline plans, but they prefer the interaction over large, small and spot plans under their power to review; (3) the compound structure of representation acts contrary to bureaucratic rationality; (4) the mode of evolving planning-policy encourages bargaining and compromise.

## Managerial Control vs. Political Conflict

The pre-1965 legal and statutory arrangements that guided planning were instituted by the British during the Mandate administration. The town planning ordinances of 1921 and 1936 provided little coordination and control. The birth of planning organizations in 1965 was related to the failures of the pre-1965 preference for a planned hierarchical settlement structure and its replacement, due to market forces, by the polar model. This situation emerged in the absence of controls (which a democratic system does not provide, especially not in an open economy). By comparison, the 1965 PBL appears on the surface to be a management tool for coordination. In its formal aspect it signifies a managerial outlook to land-use planning systems and policy.

Since the 1965 PBL, planning policy activities, including those of the central government ministries, are interconnected and often subordinated to the building licensing power of the local planning organizations. An exception is a statutory arrangement that enables the Ministry of Housing to register public housing projects, which sprang up during mass emigration times, as binding plans within the limits of the cities. This often interferes with city plans. The hierarchical feature that places the appointed regional commission above the local elected commission enables ministries to attempt to influence their causes at the higher level where they have a decisional role. Similarly, the hierarchy of plans establishes a managerially coordinated binding situation. But, in fact, the local governments are represented on the regional commissions, where they are free to mobilize support for their preferences. Thus, there is a gap between what is formally prescribed by the hierarchical system of planning policy and its organizations, and the actual make-up of its membership and its political dynamics; thus formal rigidity and the implied managerial control is overcome. The actual operation of the planning organizations leaves much to open negotiation and bargaining between local and regional professionals, and the LPBC and RPBC. Formally, then, one can identify a hierarchy.

The hierarchical structure of plans and planning organizations would lead one to expect a high level of control in the formation and execution of planning policy. However, the hierarchy of planning involves political interactional elements; it does not necessarily involve a hierarchy of execution. There are numerous explanations for this situation. Firstly, a decision structure which posits actors of varied interests, differential power and motivation side-by-side, gives priority to bargaining. Secondly, even approved plans are not always viewed as a final guide for action. Deviation (special exceptions) from plan procedures encourage negotiation and bargaining. Thirdly, regional outline plans that are in force leave detailed planning to the local level. This process often reopens outline plan deviation procedures, which call for a new plan. Furthermore, the criteria for action throughout the planning system lacks the sanctions available to a hierarchical, managerial or bureaucratic structure. By focusing on the membership, structure, power, and interaction of planning organizations, the gaps between the structural prescriptive and actual political behavior may be discerned.

## Membership, Structure and Power

The structure of Israeli planning organizations is best understood by using inter-organizational structure and behavior. The NPBL, RPBL, and LPBC — the national, regional, and local planning and building commissions — are organizational sets consisting of members of formal status, each representing an organization or a local government, a professional norm, or a planning ideology/outlook. This catch-all structure includes powerful actors with a variety of loyalties, placed in a hierarchical relation to other organizations with actors of varied motivations that often match their own. Sometimes the same actors belong to different bodies; for example, the mayor of Tel Aviv (or his representative) is chairman of the LPBC, and a member of the RPBC and NPBC.

As all of the actors have a role in decisions, outcomes are subject to their relative abilities to mobilize and use political resources. Each actor aims at his own (or his organization's) definition of the public interest; outcomes depend on political skills of persuasion and coalition-building, and on the resources used in these interactions.

The chairman of the NPBC is the Minister of Interior, or his representative. Membership includes seven members of the national government or their representatives; the mayors of Israel's three largest cities (Jerusalem, Tel Aviv and Haifa); several people appointed by the Ministry of Interior — a planner, an environmental expert, an engineer, an architect, a sociologist, a mayor, a chairman of a local council, a chairman of a regional council, a representative of women's organizations, and a representative of the settlement organizations recommended by the Jewish Agency; and a representative of the Technion (Israel Institute of Technology). The NPBC combines representatives of various interests and professional backgrounds — a combination that reflects the original Knesset intention.[7]

The RPBC includes the Regional District Officer of the Ministry of Interior, and representatives of the following national ministries: Housing, Labor, Defense, Health, Agriculture,

Transportation, and Justice; a professional planner appointed by the Ministry of Interior; five representatives of local governments in the region; and a person "versed in planning...who is not a member of either the local or central governments," appointed by the Minister of Interior.

LPBCs are city councils, made up of representatives of various political parties that competed in the previous election. The LPBC operates through subcommittees for planning and building, and it is these bodies that we refer to as LPBCs. The committees consist of six members in councils with less than twenty-one members, and ten members in cities with councils of twenty-one and over.

Given the diverse and overlapping membership of the three levels of planning, one can hardly speak of a division of power. A more descriptive term is "power interdependence" (this is reminiscent of the description of the marble cake pattern of authority in the U.S. federal system).

Formally, the LPBC deals with outline plans and especially with detailed plans, building permits; it works with private and public developers. The RPBC outlines urban and rural development, agricultural areas, industrial land use and community facilities, and oversees the process of local exceptions from approved land use plans. Rules of deviations from plans are set in the 1965 PBL. The NPBC outlines land use for agriculture, industry, roads and recreation; based on population projections, it determines the size of urban and rural settlements.

This formal division creates additional decision arenas on the very subjects supposedly delegated to a lower level of planning. For example, two of the four governmental observers in the LPBC can appeal to the RPBC, which can amend or even reverse the decision of the local committee. When the RPBC considers a plan related to a locality it is obliged to hear the local town planner before making a decision, which further extends the bargaining arena.

The local planning commission (the city council) deals with outline plans; it also debates and approves all detailed decisions of its subcommittee. Decisions of the subcommittee — which naturally deals with day-to-day matters, and which reflects the political composition of the council — are binding once approved by the full local commission. But the local commission members can use the local appeal board to reactivate an issue. This situation opens the door to politics, as developers and councilmen ally on behalf of a policy course of action. Among local coalition partners there are many trade-offs on planning policy.

The RPBC hears and decides on public objections to local plans. The objection procedure is the major formal channel for public access to the decision arena, and gives citizens and developers an opportunity to participate in the planning process. The RPBC can instruct the LPBC to take a specific course of action concerning land use and land appropriation. It can also request the LPBC to provide information about (a) local planning needs, road construction plans, and open spaces; (b) the forecasted area planning needs; (c) any matter that concerns the operations of the RPBC. There is much spot planning because the binding local or regional plans are often old and highly rigid, and each change requires the activation of an entire process of plan adoption. Because the energy and cost required for spot planning is generally equal to that required for any plan change, this usually provides an incentive to bargain over each spot instead of over larger, more comprehensive changes. The Israeli system, so it appears, prefers this uncertainty and the bargaining that follows. This is another factor that modifies the formal control of the hierarchy of planning organizations.

A regional commission has discretionary power in the execution of national plans. If it fails to prepare regional plans, the national planning commission can order other bodies or individuals to prepare such plans. Similarly, when a local commission fails to prepare local plans, the regional commission can order other bodies to prepare them. The technical planning staffs of the regional commissions are employees of the Ministry of Interior in the Department of Planning. The same hierarchical-interactive elements are present in the work of the NPBC. Its national plans require a measure of coordination with others in each region; it can intervene in regional planning and can also hear appeals from the local and regional levels. Underneath the PBC are six RPBCs and 113 LPBCs.

Two contradictory approaches were present in the legislative debate that preceded the 1965 PBL. One was that the planning process should be controlled by a central government ministry; the other was that control should be in the hands of local and central political forces, which would oversee the government ministries — especially the major building entrepreneur, the Ministry of Housing. Not until the passage of the 1965 PBL did the Ministry of

Interior acquire a key position in the hierarchy of planning organizations. The 1965 law also prevented ad hoc planning and implementation by the ministry. Since 1965 (with few exceptions), all plans of all developers, both public and private, have gone through the planning organizations. The 1965 PBL gives the NPBC the power to oversee, approve, review, and recall plans; it gives LPBCs the authority to issue building and development permits. The RPBC is involved in local plans through its powers to review. The RPBC can informally reject early initiatives of local planners, and at a later stage delay and reject local plans on which local consensus was reached.

The overlapping membership of the planning organizations does not contribute to the coherent control expected from the 1965 PBL. The control potential of the hierarchical structure was offset by political features such as the representative membership structure. Overlapping and pluralistic membership resulted in a great deal of interaction: confrontation, bargaining, coalition building, and conflict resolution. Thus, a volatile and competitive planning process — a political process which determines policy outcomes — can be identified.

A key concept which explains the dynamic political process in the planning organizations is the authoritative access to planning decisions given to a variety of actors. Its effect on the politics of planning is illustrated in the discussion below, which describes the efforts of the City of Tel Aviv in its role as a developer.

### Access and Hierarchy

Four major actors have access to the planning process and to the decision-making arena where planning policy is determined: developers, planners, members of the planning committees, and the public. Their capabilities for influencing planning vary.

There are three major ways to achieve access to the planning decisional arena: (a) by formal status, (b) through the mediation of an actor with formal status, and (c) through the public's right to object to a plan. The developer, the planner and the public exercise their influence with members of the planning organizations and with the political leadership. In local matters the political leaders are the mayor, councilmen, and political parties; at the regional level, the ministries and regional planner are involved; and at the national level, the ministries and the government are involved.

In spot planning, a developer initiates a program and (along with his private consultant) negotiates with a city planner, and then with the planning organization. The public has a statutory right to raise objections with the RPBC, where it has an opportunity to influence those with a formal decision role. However, this formal entitlement to access should not be confused with political effectiveness in the planning organizations. A local government has access to the RPBC via its statutory representative, but this does not mean it will always get its way. The RPBC planners, along with the planning division of the Ministry of Interior, create upper limits for various land uses in cities (e.g., the maximum number of offices permitted in a city). Such a limit might be in line with the national policy of population dispersion, which would make it difficult for a city to force a confrontation over the issue.

But when implementation takes place, the cities may try to obtain permission to deviate from the approved limits. Often a request for a deviation is made post facto, after the deviation has taken place. Two factors account for such deviations: (1) the pressure of market forces, and (2) the universal reluctance to use sanctions, such as cutting off financial grants to the cities. The end result is that the hierarchical structure of planning foregoes its basis of control.

The upper limit policy sets the stage for conflict. When national or regional plans fix a city's population level at, say, 200,000, and the city desires a 300,000 level, the city will confront the RPBC with a demand for a higher limit. Through its political party, the city's leadership will work to influence government members in the RPBC or the NPBC to favor the city's position. The upper limit policy is a regulative function of the hierarchical structure. Although it is likely to be modified by politics, the regulative elements of the range of lower and upper policy limits introduce a measure of control to the planning hierarchy.

At the local level the LPBC has a regulative role over spot planning, detailed plans, building licensing of developers, and construction specifications. Nevertheless, several forces tend to negate a strict managerial role for the planning hierarchy. The workload encourages delays, reviews, loose regulations, and general overseemanship rather than involvement, all of which facilitates confrontation, conflict and coalition-building. The planning hierarchy's inability to offset free-market forces also contributes to its lack of control. For example, when a regional commission sets an upper level regulation for residential land use, the implication is that the LPBC will not plan beyond the assigned level — but generally this is not the case. The free market choices of individuals about where they want to live (along with tacit local encouragement), plus pressure from developers and speculators, cause limits set by the RPBC to be overlooked. In this way plan deviation procedures are activated.

## Control via Appeals, and Planning by Deviation

Control by the RPBC is achieved less by a strict hierarchy of plans than by the institutionalization of appeals and information flow. The LPBC and developers constantly appeal to the RPBC for deviations from approved plans; this body reviews the changes and in this way retains a measure of control.[8] Despite the deviations, the RPBC considers a wide scope of issues on an area-wide basis, sets upper-level limits on various land uses, regulates the local level, and serves as a forum for appeals. Thus, for example, while the RPBC may set an upper limit of, say, 7,000 offices for Tel Aviv, the detailed planning that determines where these offices are to be located is left largely to the city.[9]

The process of planning by deviation takes place when a local outline plan has no updated regional approval, or (which is more common) when there are pressures for changes in approved plans. A developer will attempt to persuade local actors (such as the mayor, councilmen and city planners) to support his spot plans in the RPBC or when his plan deviates from the local plan. An approved outline plan for a spot enables the city to issue a building permit. Examination of a typical local outline plan of Tel Aviv indicates scores of spot plans which are different from the general local outline plans.

According to the regional planner of the Tel Aviv region, the City of Tel Aviv has over 3,000 plans. However, this is not universally the case. In Holon, a city near Tel Aviv, there is generally a convergence between the outline plans and detailed plans.[10] When an outline plan has both local and regional approval, the process of deviation is rarer and more complex — since it requires extensive confrontation and persuasion at both levels.

Approved plans may be interpreted as a set of goals and rules that are likely to reduce the role of politics in planning. This is certainly a theoretical possibility, but evidence indicates that the process of deviation continues — and so does the politics of planning policy. The need for plan flexibility accounts for the persistence of planning by deviation. Deviation politics is especially apparent when outline plans are detailed. When the social or economic environment changes, deviations are often requested. For example, new construction technologies or increased land values may lead public or private developers to attempt to change the plans.

The planning organizations allow deviations because of a variety of historical factors in Israel. Old plans remain in force, and new plans do not necessarily negate old plans — unless so stated. Until 1965, planning was guided by the Town Planning Ordinances of 1921 and 1936; prior to 1921, the rules of the Ottoman Empire guided whatever planning existed. In Tel Aviv, outline plans from the 1920s and 1930s are still in force; many of them are named after their British planner, Gaddes. In the absence of an approved city outline plan, old outline plans have been the legal basis for planning. When such outline plans are changed the RPBC is supposed to approve the changes. Tel Aviv, for example, often deviates from old Gaddes plans without regional approval — which leads to *ex post facto* bargaining and confrontation with the regional level.

In 1986, Tel Aviv approved a city-wide plan for office use in various residential sections of the city — the N-plan. Its conception and principles were negotiated with the local and regional planners prior to actual planning. Because this plan is opposed by professional associations and is under protracted review by the RPBC, many people who wish to use residences commercially, which the N-plan does not allow, have appealed to the RPBC, which may approve deviations from the city's N-plan based on the old valid plans. This is done in accordance with statutory provision of the 1965 PBL. This process may be used by the RPBC to pressure the city and its LPBC to make policy changes. The need for a transition period led the mayor to make a series of allowances for deviations based on "grandfather" clauses. The response of the mayor and the local commissions to these pressures was to allow deviations until that time when the city has resolved its conflict with the RPBC and final rules have been issued.

The process of planning by deviation is determined by

systemic structural factors. Its mode of operation involves extensive bargaining and the use of political resources (including threats by developers of appeal to the Supreme Court, which cities try to avoid). There is an abundance of bargaining by all concerned. Because planning by deviation requires approval, coalition building is often involved. Essentially, the process involves the reactivation of substantive planning issues. Since the RPBC is involved in most deviations and exceptions it is provided with a high measure of control over the dynamics of planning.

Appeals take the form of an objection to a plan during its mandatory publication, as prescribed by the 1965 PBL. Appeals have to show that there will be an adverse effect on the vicinity of the area, or that there are legal or procedural flaws. The RPBC offers citizens the only meaningful way to influence planning policy. In spite of new, stricter rules of appeal issued in 1986, it gives access to any person who wishes to propose changes in a planning policy. In that a citizen approaches the RPBC after plans have already been through the local decision processes, his participation is reactive. An appeal is likely to be successful when a coalition of RPBC members seizes the opportunity of a citizen's appeal to reassess its plans and bring proposed changes to a final vote. An appeal is also a way for members of the RPBC to delay a policy by bringing it back for reconsideration. The appeal is one of the last opportunities to reactivate an issue and place it on the public agenda before a final decision is made.

The ability to influence planning policy decisions is related to the political factors of access, negotiation and bargaining, coalition building, support mobilization, and control. It is essential for an actor interested in a policy to have access (both legal and organizational) to the decision arena. To win, an actor must be able to organize a coalition and have resources to exchange. Actors with a stake in a policy can delay, interfere, and create a setting for conflict and bargaining. Thus, politics is essential for conflict resolution and domination of a policy decision. This political role was identified by Alexander, Alterman and Law-Yone (1983), who noted that one of the goals of local planning is "to serve as a forum for mediation between different group goals and for conflict resolution."[11] They pointed to the statutory opportunity to object to plans and the representative nature of the LPBC. They did not, however, undertake a political analysis.

The RPBC in Israel uses its hierarchical power to influence city land-use planning when local plans raise issues that are of concern to the various regional members. The regional commission is concerned, for example, with roads in relation to land use, with the density of a new city, or with developer-initiated housing projects.

The hierarchy of plans and planning organizations are systemic structural features that determine the nature of political relations in the LPBC, and between the RPBC and the LPBC. Nevertheless, a city's outline plan may guide its development policies without having regional approval, or a developer can approach the RPBC and attempt to have his plans approved on the basis of an old plan that has regional recognition, and which the local level considers irrelevant.

Lastly, it is important to underscore that systemic structural features mandate bargaining and negotiation, which is facilitated by the hierarchical structure of planning organizations. These features have ramifications in yet another feature of planning, namely the betterment tax, which accompanies changes in the value of land. The betterment tax was discretionary up to 1982. It encouraged entrepreneurs to deviate from building permits, often with the support of the local authorities themselves. Documents and protocols of the Jerusalem planning commission indicate that when a major hotel was being built in the center of Jerusalem, developers built over 7000 sq. ft. beyond the approved plans and went so far as to infringe on a public park. In the RPBC, the city representatives noted that the municipality would not sue the developer — as they should have done according to the 1965 PHL — but would request a formal spot change to a legally-binding plan. In this way the municipality would be able to collect the betterment tax.[12] This procedure not only serves as a basis for breaking the law by government authorities, but the betterment tax also provides a convenient setting for bargaining for benefits distribution. Prior to 1982, the exact amount to be paid was negotiated by city officials and developers. A municipal court commented on this process: "...for years the developer deviated from the permit. The local planning commission was aware of this, but did nothing to halt the illegal construction...in changing a non-commercial designation to a commercial one."[13]

It appears, then, that the betterment tax on changes in land-use plans also contributed to local planning by deviation. The tax is an important factor in the study of planning because it reflects on the administrative culture and planning policy implementation, and highlights the power of economic considerations in planning.

In 1982, the betterment tax was reassessed. A legal reform and amendment to the 1965 PBL made tax rates clear, mandatory and not amenable to bargaining or discretion.[14] This procedure modified irregular behavior by developers and local government, but the inclination for spot planning goes on and indirectly it yields betterment revenues.

## Hierarchical Planning Levels

In the planning organizations, influence can be wielded at various stages and in various relationships: such as among planners of all levels, when there is information flow, and when legal controversies arise. Of importance is the appeal stage, when a member of the regional commission files an appeal — usually on behalf of a personal, public or private interest. The appeal stage opens the way for objections to plans. It gives the public a chance to delay or modify a policy. Thus they can bargain with a city's mayor or councilmen in the LPBC. And if they cannot get satisfaction there, they can object and appeal to the RPBC. Mayors usually enter an appeal fray with all the support and resources they can muster, because it is a political struggle for domination of the power relationships and influence over substantive decisions.

Objections create long delays, but they generate a process of reaffirmation, modification, or negation. The procedure formally begins when a city deposits plans in the RPBC for public assessment. However, under threat of an objection, a city can postpone the deposit and attempt to resolve the conflict with the objector. A trade-off allows the city to avoid delays, the developer to put his capital to work, and the objector to get some satisfaction. When there are many objections to a plan (either legitimate or as a delaying tactic), the city or developer may attempt to bring the issue to a head in a confrontation; then a process of coalition-building takes place among the involved parties in the final arena — the RPBC.

To demonstrate these roles, and the role of the RPBC as a forum for appeals and public participation, we shall analyze briefly the conflict[15] over a development project in the City of Tel Aviv: the Golda Meir Center.

The City of Tel Aviv was the developer of a 35-acre planning project in the center of the city. Given that the entire land reserve of the city is low, this was rightly viewed as a major undertaking.

The city had an edge over private developers because it faced few local restraints. The initial ideas and guidelines given to the private planning consultant came from the city (particularly from the mayor and from the City Development Corporation). Thus responsibility for initial planning was confined to a narrow circle of people. Support of the LPBC was achieved with relative ease. As the development would memorialize the name of the Labor party's late prime minister, the support of Labor members was facilitated. The Likud (the major component of the municipal coalition) followed the lead of Mayor Lahat, and the deputy mayor, who was chairman of the LPBC.

The city acted as both the planning authority and the developer. When objections to the plan arose the city made changes to forestall some of the debate in the RPBC. After the plan was deposited the commission issued a call for public objections. The city then attempted to block the process and reach agreement with the objectors, but it did not succeed.

The project — which involved an extension of the city's Museum of Arts compound — would use the 35 acres for public activities, thus replacing the undeveloped open space in the area. The land use agreed upon in the LPBC included two acres for about 200 dwelling units. The residential construction would be auctioned off to a builder, who would finance the public amenities by utilizing the extended building rights allotted by the LPBC. This practice of providing a developer with increased construction rights in exchange for development is common.

In the case of the Golda Meir Center there were two types of appeals. One was by residents of the area; the people's right to appeal local planning decisions to the RPBC is statutorily assured by the 1965 PBL. Another appeal was by members of the RPBC; according to item 11.d of the 1965 PBL, each member of the RPBC has the right to reopen discussions on a subject decided on by a subcommittee.

The RPBC hearing focused on both procedural and substantive issues. The first question was procedural: Was the agenda to be the citizens' objections or the city's appeal? Objections are dealt with in the full RPBC, while appeals are handled separately. It was ruled that the hearing was for objections. One objector requested that the minutes indicate that the notice of the meeting was sent to him at such a late date that he did not have sufficient time for proper preparation; this was done to provide the basis for a possible future appeal to the NPBC or to the Supreme Court. Such threats are used to influence an opponent to modify his position.

Members of the RPBC also delayed decisions, and requested a repeat of the discussion; at the same time, public objections were heard.

## Coalition Influence

Two coalitions emerged in the RPBC, which was to decide on the Golda Meir development project. One coalition included organizations outside the region, such as the Nature Protection Society; the other coalition included the mayors of the region, who were mobilized by the mayor of Tel Aviv. The mayors usually send their representatives to the RPBC; however, when conflict emerges and a city has a high stake in an issue, the mayors themselves are mobilized. Together, they wield extensive influence. Although the mayor of Tel Aviv and the other four mayors in the Tel Aviv RPBC belong to different political parties, on important issues in the RPBC, they band together vis-a-vis the government's representatives. At other times they may form other coalitions.

The objecting coalition of the Nature Protection Society and the representative of the Environmental Protection Service were joined by residents of the area. Together they raised the issue of overbuilding at the expense of public green areas. They also pointed to a procedural flaw in the plan publication, and brought up a purely technical flaw — a discrepancy of one-eighth of an acre between the planning script and the published plans. Other points raised by the objectors were the omission of a topographical map in the plan, the argument that putting a swimming pool near a religious high school would offend modesty, and the fact that an existing neighborhood park would be eliminated (the last point would attract the attention and support of the nature preservation vote and ecology supporters). To the Ministry of Interior representatives, the objectors pointed out that no city money was available for development, and hence no commitment should be made.

The objectors wanted open space, no construction, a club for religious youth, and the extension of the nearby religious school. But since the local commission had decided to go ahead with the development project, the objectors tried to reverse the local decision at the regional level. The legal argument that not enough time had been given to publication and public review of the plan drew the support of the Ministry of Justice. Although the argument was not accepted by the chairman, the ministry joined the opposition coalition.

The coalition in support of the local development policy was headed by the mayor of Tel Aviv, who arrived with his legal staff, city planners, the private planning consultant who had prepared the plan, the director of the city's development corporation, and an assortment of other advisors. The city argued primarily on the merits of the plan. Its argument focused on the preservation of open space as the key element. The mayor's strong commitment to the project made him use all available resources in an attempt to dominate the conflict. He launched a campaign to discredit the objectors and exhibited a model showing that high percentages of the project were devoted to public use. The amount of residential construction was less than in previous drafts of the plan; there was space for walking, and recreation space for mothers and children in the public squares. The planners pointed out that the plan had been under discussion for twelve years, during which time many changes were made; only half an acre of commercial use had been added, mainly to finance the development of the open space.

The coalitions appeared to be evenly matched if the matter should come to a vote. The following tactic was then used by the mayor. He introduced a document signed by the major public objector to the plan, in which the objector agreed to drop his objections in return for the mayor meeting certain of his demands. In the document, the director of the City Development Corporation agreed to the objector's demands that the city not relocate the religious school that was in the neighborhood, and that the city provide financial support for a religious youth center and expand the curriculum of the school from one to four years. The mayor's purpose in publicizing the document was to persuade the undecided members of the RPBC that the objector was not acting in good faith, but was trying to obtain benefits for his interests, rather than to improve the planning policy.

Thus the objector was forced to defend himself rather than his objections. He explained that many pressures had been exerted on him by various city emissaries — including a noted attorney and a former ministry director-general. The director of the City Development Corporation had approached him on behalf of the mayor, so he argued, and the common practice of bargaining had taken place. The objector said that the document read at the meeting had been suggested by the mayor's representative. He even claimed that threats had been made against him.

The objector was discredited by the mayor's claim that his objections had been merely to achieve benefits, even though the

chairman of the RPBC ruled that the document reflected a legitimate bargaining procedure between adversaries in the planning
process. However, the sense of the meeting was that the objector
had done something improper. In a last effort to reactivate the opposition coalition, he argued for preservation of the natural sur-
roundings of groves and trees. In this he was supported by the environmental organizations, which demanded a reduction in the
open parking areas, as well as in the residential and commercial
areas. The Nature Protection Society focused its opposition on the
danger to a few old trees in the area of the project. Along with the
objector, the society agreed that the religious school in the area
would be disturbed by the project.

As expected, the mayors supported the development. They
pointed to the economic benefits of the project, and protested
against the delaying tactics which caused a loss of tax money and
prevented Tel Aviv's progress. The deputy-mayor of Tel Aviv
agreed to compensate for the elimination of the park and trees in
the area by stepping up the completion of a large park in a less-af-
fluent area in the south of the city. The mayors emphasized that the
project's self-financing nature was a laudable approach to development in view of the city's stringent situation. Furthermore, they
argued, open parking would bring crowds and business, while
indoor parking was too expensive and not used by the public.

The outcome came through the resolution of procedural and
substantive matters. The procedural flaw in the time allocated for
publication and review of the plans was noted, but it did not block
the final substantive decision. The RPBC voted to disallow the objections to the plan's small extension of residential and business
areas, and turned down a proposal that the plan be returned to the
city. The deciding votes came from the mayors, along with the
representative of the government's Land Management Authority
(whose interest is development).

## Theoretical Implications

This brief analysis of the development policy of the City of Tel
Aviv points to a number of political elements in the planning process:

1. A procedural hierarchy affects substantive policy, the political
   behavior of the members of the RPBC, and the nature of appeals
   and public objections.

2. During attempts to dominate decisions on planning policy, the hierarchical structure makes salient the use of political resources. These resources include the ability to engage in delaying tactics, which facilitates the realignment of coalitions. The delaying tactics and coalition-building politics run counter to prevalent notions of efficient and expeditious planning. Here we attribute delays to the inextricable role of politics in planning policy.
3. Access to planning decisions is empirically identifiable. Thus, it is an important analytical category in the role of politics in planning policy. It is discernable in the process of coalition-building in the planning organizations.
4. Volitant coalition-building is another political category. It is derived from the need for domination of conflicts in planning policy, because conflicts must be resolved by a decision. Coalitions are based on a variety of motivations, both procedural and substantive; they change when actors have different stakes in an issue.
5. Mobilization is a third political category which aids the explanation of planning policy. It is related to coalition-building among those who have access to decisions in the planning organizations.
6. In the conflict over planning policy, political resources are activated and exchanged.

It can be argued that although planning organizations are hierarchically structured, they do not provide the expected control. Mitigating factors are the structural provision for intervention in local planning policy, appeal objections, and shifting coalitions. Thus, notwithstanding the delays in planning due to conflict, control is achieved through planning by deviation and the political process of conflict resolution.

## The Setting of Planning Policy

To what extent is the planner involved in the politics of planning policy? What is his or her role in local and regional planning organizations, in the networks of relationships which accompany conflict over planning policy, and in central-local relations? What is the planner's role in planning policy conflict resolution? And what can be said about the planner's political and professional role in the context of the planning structures? In answering these questions we explicate on the role and extent of influence of planners in the decision process of the planning organizations. Can the planner be compared to the bureaucrat who wields influence via control of information flow, use of discretion, and the setting of alternatives for the public agenda and decision-making forums? What is crucial for our analysis is to analyze what happens with planners when they have access — statutorily and behaviorally — to planning decision arenas such as the LPBC and the RPBC.

We begin by showing a strong, albeit rare, stand of a local planner vis-a-vis a mayor, and proceed to consider planners' areas of influence. We then analyze his role in the hierarchy of plans and his position in a given administrative-political structure.

## Planner and Mayor

In major planning policies the mayor and a political coalition on the LPBC will determine planning policy. A mayor may choose to use a private planning consultant, who is usually an architect. A mayor's involvement and the direction of a planning policy or a project can be done with or without the cooperation of the local planner. The development of the seashore of Tel Aviv is an uncharacteristic example of where the local planner took a political position against the mayor. The seashore plan included provisions for the development of a public bathing area, a number of high-rise hotels, a communal area, restaurants and cafes, entertainment and recreation facilities, a limited number of expensive "prestigious" dwelling units, and drainage infrastructure.[16] The mayor brought in private planning consultants. The local planner, attempting to assure his role in supervising and reviewing the development, attempted to gain support of an opposition coalition within the LPBC and eventually fought the plan in the RPBC. In order to achieve a reviewer status, he attempted to influence the decision-making process of the local and regional planning commissions. By confronting the private planners, the local planner took up a position against the planning goals as outlined by the mayor. The question to be addressed is how far the planner carried this struggle given the systemic limitations on his role, and the fact that the private planners in charge of the project were under the direction of the mayor.

The local planner's challenge to the planning approach made the private planner more active in the politics of planning than is usually the case. In the planning of the Tel Aviv seashore, the private planners, on behalf of the mayor, had to attempt to convince members of the local government and the local planning commission of the merits of the plan, and that the goals implied in the plans were actually that of the mayor. The local coalition structure was used by the various contestants. The actions of the planners among the city council members were mainly directed toward the opposition party which could, through criticism of the proposed high-rise hotels on the seashore, create a public uproar that might hinder implementation of the plan. (Criticism centered on the fact that construction would block the fresh westerly wind into the city, thus seriously affecting the environment.) Furthermore, the private planners, taking advantage of internal disagreements, attempted to seek approval of the plan in the small planning department of the City of Tel Aviv. The aim was to have the mayor's plan accepted; a subsidiary political aim was, of course, to bypass the local planner, who was the professional reviewer of plans.

The local planner of Tel Aviv, a civil servant, in providing advice and information, has a key policy role in the LPBC of the City of Tel Aviv. When the plan was presented to the LPBC, many of its key features were opposed: the high-rise hotels along the seashore, the high population density envisioned for the area, and the projected major transportation artery along the seashore, which would have the effect of separating a projected boardwalk from the seashore itself. The planner, a woman, was the only planner of high enough status and seniority potentially able to delay the mayor's efforts for quick approval of the development project; she was among the few who challenged the implications of the plan.[17] The efforts of the city planner to influence policy indicated a keen political approach. Using representatives of the opposition faction on the LPBC, the planner was invited by them to report on the plan. She first approached the mayor for permission to address the opposition parties. Her action came at a time when the plan was to be considered by the LPBC and then by the RPBC. Such meetings would receive press coverage and could create further delays or new opposition. In spite of the local planner's unusual opposition to the seashore plan, the mayor charged the planner with the responsibility of presenting the plan to the RPBC, as was common practice. To have used the planning consultant instead would have created immediate procedural and substantive confrontation. At first the planner refused to follow the mayor's directive; she opposed several major features of the plan and felt that it would be inappropriate to stand before the regional commission to seek acceptance of it on behalf of the city. But like any bureaucrat involved in major policies, the choice was clear. At the mayor's insistence the planner went before the regional commission. There, although she did not oppose the plan in formal sessions, she could speak freely to the regional planners about her reservations, which coincided with some of the reservations of the regional planners.[18]

Sending the city's planner, who had reservations about the plan to the regional commission, was a calculated risk. Had the local planner not presented the plan to the regional commission, her absence would have been too obvious and could have become a major issue by those who opposed the plan, including the press. Given the mayor's commitment to the plan, the local planner was unlikely to go into an all-out fight against it, unless she was willing to risk her reputation, if not her position altogether — something planners are not too keen on doing. When a plan is highly valued by the key local political figure, the planner cannot be effective. A planner's behavior is likely to be modified and his opposition overcome via the administrative managerial structure.

Planners at the regional planning commissions can affect decisions because they have statutory access to the decision-making process. Their capacity to influence decisions is like that of other decision makers on the commission. Their potential role is important, but their actual role in determining planning policy will depend on their ability to activate resources, join in coalitions, and have a stand which does not generate strong conflict.

The regional planner is the key planning professional in the RPBC, where local plans come for approval. The office is linked to the planning and administrative structure of the Ministry of Interior. The variety of membership means that conflict is a part of the RPBC; the role of the regional planner is, therefore, potentially influential. When a planning conflict occurs in the RPBC it is the regional planner and the planning department of the Ministry of Interior who are strongly involved. If a regional planner sees in a local plan regional implications, it might be a cause for conflict. Similarly, the practice of local planning by deviation (from old or newly approved plans) is also the setting for information flow, appeals and conflict at both local and regional levels. Indeed, conflict might ensue from a combination of the above.

The planning policy for the Tel Aviv seashore reflected the above situation. The major concern was for the degree of convergence of the seashore plan with the regional planning conceptions. The regional planners and the planner of the Ministry of Interior ordered the formation of review teams to examine the plan.[19] Each actor set forth arguments relevant to his particular organizational framework. The planners of the Ministry of Interior referred to national planning goals and argued that: (1) extensive development of Tel Aviv would prevent effective implementation of the national population dispersal policy; (2) extensive hotel building would require an additional work force which would further attract people to the city; (3) the development of Tel Aviv into a major tourist center would take place at the expense of other less prosperous regions of the country. Environmental arguments were also put forward: (1) the proposed highway along the beach might create a serious air flow problem, and (2) the highrise hotels would prevent westerly winds from penetrating the city.[20] The regional planning position was close to that of the city planner and clearly against the mayor's plan. The regional planner joined in arguing these professional planning issues, and did so more vigorously than other members of the RPBC. A regional planner may not always be able to lead a winning coalition, but he can certainly delay a decision. For example, part of the plan called for a drainage strip about 80 meters out to sea. The regional planner proposed that this feature be further assessed by experts and that models be made. The planner from the Ministry of Interior also delayed the project by inquiring into the environmental impact of the plan and how the plan would be integrated with all seashore plans for the region.

The mayor's planning consultant who prepared the plan had to defend it after the city planner presented it. Thus, the planning conflict was mainly between professionals over technical and procedural matters. The issue of long-range goals was neglected. The conflict resolution would remain in the hands of others in the RPBC, who may or may not be affected by the procedural argumentation. Procedural features emphasized by the planners meant that the politics of planning policy was left to others. Thus, the planners affected substantive planning matters only indirectly. The planner's technical approach is illustrated in the response of the consultant planner to whether their plan coincided with plans for the region as a whole: "A municipal corporation gave us guidelines. Members of the program committee were representatives of the City of Tel Aviv, Tourism Ministry and Treasury. Their program served as a basis for our plan."[21] The controversy in the regional commission makes it clear that planners who work for an organization — such as a local government, a mayor, or a ministry — serve that organization's interests. Professional planners who are part of a planning organization such as the RPBC tend to act like other decision makers; they add their professional perspective to the process. Regional planners are generally more willing and able to take a stand in confrontations with local planners, local governments or its mayors.

## Local Planners' Influence

An important area of influence left to the local planners is the domain of initiating changes in land-use plans. This procedural action has important substantive ramifications and is likely to affect planning goals. When a change of land designation involves those with a formal role in planning, a planner is likely to have to take a back seat in any emerging controversy. But in the many activities that do not raise a strong political conflict, the planner's role is dominant. The local planner may succeed in convincing a mayor or the LPBC to change land designation and to pay the required compensation to owners. Land-use designation change is always related to a plan in force. Change of land designation has social and economic significance. A planner who responds to market forces may support an area's designation from low to high density, and thus increase the value of the land. He may approach the planning of an area with sensitivity to the less affluent. This can be done in the various levels of planning: in the outline plan or detailed plan, or by planning by deviation. Housing in a high cost neighborhood may be planned for large residences (around 200 sq. meters) or to combine large and small residences, in this way affecting social class integration. The local planner is thereby open to pressure from entrepreneurs and speculators. He may respond by using his close ties with the LPBC to reject such plans.

The regional planner is another important actor in land designation decision processes and especially in the local process of planning by deviation. For example, a change in a detailed plan of a housing project located in the expensive north Tel Aviv area was brought before the LPBC. The recommendation of the city planner was to approve large area apartments (approx. 180 square meters) in a group of six buildings, which were previously planned as low cost 80 square meter apartments. The argument behind the proposed change in designation was that the builder had difficulties in selling the smaller apartments. While the LPBC approved the change, the regional planner thought that "social considerations" should not have been neglected. He thought that small and large apartments would be the better mix.[22] His social view of planning was materialized by delaying approval of the plan in the RPBC. Such power is used from time to time to set limits on the size of apartments in cities. In the politics of planning a mayor who leads a policy of development can overcome social considerations. A striking example of this occurred in Jerusalem. Until 1967 the area of Yemin Moshe housed less wealthy people. Following the Six Day War this area, with its panoramic view of the Old City, was turned into a high cost residential area. The municipal corporation evacuated and compensated the poorer population; more affluent people moved in, in this way benefitting from the huge public reconstruction investment.

It is difficult to generalize about the intensity of a political economy approach or social considerations present in planning and by planners. Variations in approach characterize the process. We can state with assurance that when a political leadership is behind a social or non-social planning approach, that approach is likely to dominate. Similarly, a planner's social or non-social planning approach is dominant when there is no salient political controversy and when planners are left to wield influence in the RPBC or with the mayor.

Unlike the city planner, the regional planner often finds himself in the position of a political broker — a key position in instances of change in land-use designation. His alliance is sought by the city's planners and political leadership because he or she is in a position to influence members of the regional commission, at least in non-controversial matters, when they have little information at their disposal. The hierarchical structure of planning organizations becomes, then, a setting for the politics of planning policy. The regional planner's broker role between a city and members of the regional commission creates a setting of trade-offs, which benefit professional planning considerations. The regional planner's ability to influence planning decisions is also enhanced by the general absence of approved regional outline plans. When such plans are in effect the planner has the power to initially legitimize the practice of planning of deviation. This process gives expression to a major feature of the Israeli administrative culture, namely negotiation and bargaining, which has not escaped planning even though planning is a most regulated and legally organized activity.

Having noted the structural and behavioral factors that are likely to increase the political role of the regional planner, we should also underscore the fact that even without the regional planner, a mayor of a large city such as Jerusalem or Tel Aviv is still capable of mobilizing support on the regional commission (and capable of overcoming opposition by a regional planner). But this task is significantly more difficult and a mayor would take into account his long-term dependence on the regional planner (but this is not the case with the local planner).

## Planners' Professional Role, and the Hierarchy of Plans

The Israeli administrative-political setting gives local and regional planners opportunities to become involved in planning policy because they are positioned at key junctures in the central-local relationship of ministerial, municipal and regional levels. Within the local or regional planning hierarchy, the planner can hire staff for plan preparation, and review and supervise consultants who are commissioned to do city planning. As reviewer and overseer of local plans, the planner can provide or withhold additional information so as to influence the decision-making process. The planner can also contribute to the setting of the agenda and the determination of the planning policy timetable. However, planners in Israel are a part of the local administrative (political) hierarchy and are thus very likely to serve the mayor, notwithstanding their professional position.

These structural features lead one to the conclusion that, like the bureaucrat, the planner has high potential of influence over planning activity and policy. The planner can be distinguished from the bureaucrat because: (1) his role in implementation is more limited, given the role of developers (private and public) in this domain; and (2) unlike the bureaucrat the planner is directly supervised by the mayor, as head of the administrative hierarchy, and by a political coalition of the commission (LPBC). The key question is: Is the planner's professional standing a resource in planning conflicts when other actors of the LPBC, and others with access and roles in planning decisions and arenas, also have a high stake in a planning policy?

The planner is professionally involved in the preparation of master plans (which are not legally binding), and outline and detailed plans (which are legally binding). The growing tendency to leave outline plans broad gives the planner a role in project and in spot planning. Where approved outline plans exist the local planner affects the policy agenda by controlling the information about specific building plans, and the relation of local outline plans or detailed plan to regional plans. When updated regional plans are not available — as is the case in many regions in Israel — the planner, along with the LPBC's legal advisor, is involved in determining the legality of specific project plans and whether they are congruent with existing (usually old) plans. Here also lies a limitation on the planner. He may urge that they approve the spot planning (which reflects new planning) and direct the spot plan for approval at the regional level. The developer may support this course of action and what follows is the process of planning by deviation. The planner thus has a key role in moving for changes. Much of the spot planning undertaken in Israel ultimately involves a change in the legal status of plans, a factor that encourages deviation and interaction among actors. For example, of 888 plans developed in Jerusalem between 1959 and 1974, 68 percent were detailed plans and 31.4 percent represented changes or deviations from approved outline plans. The planner's efforts may also be thwarted; a developer may choose to adhere to the old binding plan and reject the city planner's attempt to update the plans. LPBC members may also take an active role in this process, as well as the members of the RPBC. In these instances the planner plays a key role in providing information and recommending alternatives to the LPBC. Because of his interactive and dependent relations with the regional level, he is likely to do this in coordination with the regional planner.

When a plan is brought before the local planning commission by a private planner, the city planners exercise three distinct roles: (1) communication with the private planner, (2) technical guidance and information, and (3) guidance and influence on the decision of the local commission. The local planner generally participates in the interaction. Using information as his major resource, he influences the nature of the decisions taken regarding a plan. In the planning of new areas that have no approved outline plans (and therefore stand on shaky legal footing) the planner can influence decisions. Formally, the absence of an outline plan indicates an absence of an official intention or goal for the land under consideration. More importantly, it gives local planners a chance to intervene and shape an issue under discussion. Planners attempt to introduce a measure of rationality, updating and a more comprehensive coordinative approach to planning. In non-conflict issues they are likely to achieve these goals.

## Concluding Note

What characterizes the role of the city planner and regional planner is their common ability to raise professional considerations, and in this way obstruct the otherwise highly politicized planning process. The regional planner has the more influential role in planning politics. Given the political structure of the local and regional planning organizations, and the roles played by a variety of actors (notably, a city's political leadership), planners are basically bound and constrained by the organizations in which they function. Congruence between the profession of planning and the politics of planning is difficult to achieve. The nature of the local planning arena, however, is political and short-term. Planners are often required to respond to political demands for spot plans or project plans, which call for quick results if not the negation of professional considerations. The regional planner, in his key position, is also constrained. Juxtaposed with his proclivity for a long-term comprehensive approach, his other roles of approving, hearing appeals etc., are limiting. In preparing the regional outline plan he or she can adopt a broader perspective. The hierarchical structure of planning was intended to create a high measure of congruity between city outline and project plans, and regional outline plans. The regional planner's role is strengthened by the lack of a coherent hierarchy of approved plans. It gives him an additional role as a broker between city leadership and the RPBC. This short-term need is not the best of professional planning standards, but it has been the reality in Israel for the past 40 years. It most certainly places regional planners at the center of controversy and influence.

On the local scene, assertion of professional norms by

planners is limited although not insignificant. When a mayor's goals are clearly stated, local planners can do little to affect the course of events. The clientele for the local planner is the mayor and the LPBC. He contributes to the formulation of goals within the administrative structure. But local planners, or planners from the Ministry of Housing, for example, cannot go public. Planners cannot deviate from the ministry's policy goals. In the RPBC the regional planner has a stronger role in decision making and in public appearances, but he is more limited within the organizational setting of the Ministry of Interior.

To conclude, where planners are a part of a local hierarchical framework, their role can be limited; where they are given a role in enactment, they can be expected to advance their professional point of view. There are limits imposed by the interactive multi-organizational structure of the planning organization's hierarchy. A local planner enjoys technical and prompting roles, while the regional planner's role is predominantly political (because he or she is a part of the approval and enactment process in the RPBC). Regional and local planners may act on behalf of political leadership and private and public entrepreneurs.

Advocacy planning, or a political economy approach to planning, cannot be taken on by a local planner publicly, although within his administrative setting he certainly proposes and attempts to convince in this vein. As we shall see later (in chapter 4), in one instance aid was given by a regional planner to a local community leadership in their bargaining with the CPAL. This was a clear case of a coordinated administrative position to support a community plan because of social considerations.

Lastly, the public has only meager contacts with planners or the planning process. When all the plans between 1959 and 1974 were examined, it was found that the major group of people who appealed and expressed legal objections during the plan deposit period were landowners (59.9 percent) and representatives of the Land Management Authority (11.8 percent). Furthermore, 75 percent of those who challenged planning decisions were people who resided in well-to-do neighborhoods (i.e., from high socioeconomic backgrounds).[23]

We have shown how a variety of systemic, structural and normative features affect the role of planners. The key finding is that planners are a part of the administrative political structure and may therefore be viewed as having a similar sort of influence that bureaucrats have on policy in a given system. The special professional aspect of planners bears on policy when a planner is administratively placed in a mediating position between the local government and the planning organizations.

# Notes — Chapter 3

1. Hanf, K. and Scharpf, F.W. *Interorganizational Policy Making.* London: Sage, 1978.
2. McAuslan, P. *The Ideologies of Planning Law.* Oxford: Pergamon, 1980.
3. A theoretical effort in the study of implementation is Alterman, R. "Implementation Analysis in Urban and Regional Planning: Toward a Research Agenda" in Healey, P., McDougall, G. and Thomas, M.J. *Planning Theory.* Oxford: Pergamon, 1982, pp. 225-245.
4. Wright, E.O. *Class Crisis and the State.* London: New Left Books, 1978; Dunleavy, D.J. *Urban Political Analysis.* London: Macmillan, 1980; and O'Connor, J. *The Fiscal Crisis of the State.* New York: St. Martin, 1973.
5. Blowers, A. *The Limits of Power: The Politics of Local Planning.* Oxford: Pergamon, 1980; and "Much Ado About Nothing?. A Case Study of Planning and Power" in Healey, *et al.*, 1980, pp. 140-160.
6. Ministry of Interior, Planning and Building Law, 1985.
7. *Ibid.* and State of Israel, *Knesset Proceedings*, Vol. 43. Jerusalem, 1965 (Hebrew).
8. The practice of planning and implementation by deviation has been noted by Alexander, E.R., Alterman, R. and Law-Yone, H. "Evaluating Plan Implementation: The National Statutory Planning System in Israel" in Diamond, D. and McLaughlin (eds.) *Progress in Planning* 20. Oxford: Pergamon, 1983, pp. 97-172.
9. Interview with D. Radosher, regional planner, and *Minutes*, RPBC, Tel Aviv (4 January 1987).
10. *Ibid.*
11. Alexander, Alterman, and Law-Yone (1983), p. 132.
12. *Minutes*, RPBC — Jerusalem (19 December 1974).
13. Municipal Court — Jerusalem (5 October 1975).
14. Ministry of Interior, PBL 1965, Third Amendment, p. 76.
15. The following discussion indicates the process of planning policy decisions. It is based on participation-observation at the meetings, the minutes, and interviews with participants.
16. *Minutes*, RPBC — Tel Aviv 83b (17 February 1971), p. 27.
17. Interview with council members, the planner O. Kirshman, and *Minutes*, RPHC — Tel Aviv 172 (11 September 1972).

18. *Ibid.*
19. Memo of E. Brutskus, Planner, Ministry of Interior RPHC — file (12 December 1972).
20. *Minutes*, RPBC — Tel Aviv 172 (11 September 1972).
21. *Ibid.*, p. 1.
22. Interview with D. Radosher, regional planner of the Tel Aviv RPBC (3 March 1987).
23. Cf: Alexander, Alterman, and Law-Yone (1983), esp. p. 138.

# Chapter 4

# NORMATIVE DETERMINANTS
# OF PLANNING POLICY

Urban growth and primacy emerged in Israel mainly by market forces and in the setting of a dominant rural ideology of structured interests, one manifestation of which is the Committee for the Preservation of Agricultural Land (CPAL). Discussion centers on how the non-urban ideology and its organizational manifestation, the CPAL, deals with dynamic urban development. A historical view of the effect of systemic normative features on planning and development policy is given in chapter 2. The CPAL influences land-use and urban planning policy by having the power to (1) set the rules of the game, and (2) set the allocative procedures, including a veto power over land use. These roles are viewed as structural policy in the domain of planning and it directly affects the politics of planning policy.

In the many policy categories in the literature there is a distinction between allocative, and structural or regulatory policies. The former includes decision processes which confer benefits (material or symbolic); the latter includes frameworks and policies, including authority, structures, or rules to guide future allocations. Salisbury has noted that "regulatory policies impose constraints on subsequent behavior...and thus indirectly deny or confirm potentially beneficial options."[1] The CPAL is exclusionary. As a decision set it can confer (or withhold) benefits upon individuals, groups and communities through its approval and licensing power. Being involved in both domains allows it to create an interactive system between patterns of demands, strategies and activated resources.[2] The CPAL faces a highly fragmented demand pattern — demands are made by individuals, investors, land developers, and municipal governments.

## Procedural and Structural Policy

The CPAL's role in structural and allocative polices may be analyzed in terms of its rule-making procedures. Structural policy, which is the basis for the CPAL's allocative capacity to confer or withhold benefits, stems from the 1965 National Planning and Building Law (PBL). But policy is also determined through it as a policy forum where rules are evolved. An organization's capacity to set structural policy gives a clue as to its influence. Whereas a statute law provides for the broad framework for action, it is rule setting by a decision unit that is likely to determine the nature of outcomes. Rules not only provide for the ability of an organization to protect itself from encroachments, but also gives it enough flexibility so that it can remain the focal point in the decision-making process. Nevertheless, as part of the political process, bargaining occurs, and this often leads to gross deviations from procedure. The CPAL follows this pattern.

The CPAL has its origin in the recognition that urban development is a powerful force which can shape the face of a society. Historically, the planned agricultural settlements were a reflection of a policy of the power structure and its dominant ideology, namely the strategy of Jewish settlement in Palestine. The national elite was heavily dominated by Labor movement rural interests.[3] Agricultural settlements such as kibbutzim and moshavim benefited from national support under Labor rule, and this enabled them to survive in the face of massive industrialization development. It was essential for them to have leverage points in the social and political system, and the CPAL was such a leverage point. Formal statements of CPAL proponents view the review body as a means of assuring the country a basis for food subsistence; while others attempt to place its role in the framework of garden-city, green belt, or open space preservation concepts. But a brief glance at its membership composition is sufficient to discard these arguments as secondary in favor of a political-policy interpretation: the CPAL is an organizational manifestation of a systemic power distribution, and manipulation of ideology in favor of groups and organizations. While it influences urban planning and development, these are not its major concerns. The CPAL is located in the planning hierarchy in order that it be assured a political role.

Before the 1965 PBL an interministerial committee performed some of the functions that the CPAL has performed since then. The importance of the CPAL to urban planning cannot be overstated, especially for the large urban centers whose land reserves are small, and where development has to encroach on agricultural land (see chapter 6).

The potential influence of the CPAL on planning and urban development lies in the constraints it places on the statutory planning organizations, and their susceptibility to CPAL rule-making and veto power. Conflict with the CPAL results from pressure by developers, cities or ministries that wish to develop agricultural land for urban purposes. The confrontations which the CPAL is involved in makes it directly involved in urban planning and a determinant of its decisions.

The preservation of agricultural land is noted in key parts of the 1965 PBL. Article 49 (Item 1) states that national outline plans shall "prescribe the purposes to which land shall be assigned, and the use thereof, while safeguarding the designation for agricultural purposes suitable land...."[4] Similar guidelines were made for local and regional outline plans. The national outline plans specify the right to issue rules concerning the preservation of agricultural land, recreation, and afforestation. The regional outline plans specify afforestation; local outline plans deal with open space. Even though the preservation of agricultural land is clearly distinguished from the concept of open space, the CPAL is capable of influencing the use of both at all planning levels.

The first amendment to the PBL concerned how the land is to be designated as agricultural and when it could be released for urban development. The amendment specifically names the CPAL and makes the following provisions: (1) the CPAL [is provided] with the authority to declare land as agricultural "on the basis of the opinion of a committee of experts that is appointed by the Minister of Agriculture."[5] The regulation does not, however, clearly define agricultural land. Rather, it defines non-agricultural functions and purposes as "construction or land-use which is not directly required for agricultural production or cultivation or for raising livestock";[6] (2) rules of operation for the CPAL are determined by itself; (3) the CPAL is authorized to review plans at national, regional and local levels. Its approval is required on any urban plans that outline future physical development on agricultural land; it can veto plans dealing with agricultural land; and plans designating projects situated on agricultural land may have their relevant permits withheld by planning organizations, including the CPAL. Finally, urban plans made on non-agricultural land, which is subsequently designated as agricultural, can be changed or cancelled only at the CPAL's discretion. Thus, the areas left open to CPAL interaction with the planning organizations and developers are numerous. To make a change of land designation the CPAL is regulated so that it cannot merely respond to urban needs, it has to go through a procedure of designation change. Because the CPAL can statutorily determine its own mode of operation there is a theoretical likelihood that no changes will take place. Yet, the CPAL does influence urban planning policy.

The sectorial bias of the CPAL can be seen in the composition of its membership. Agricultural representation dominates, while the urban sector has but one direct representative. Moreover, the law stipulates that a representative of local authorities shall be appointed by the Minister of Interior. But this reference does not necessarily imply a local urban government representative; conceivably, the Minister could appoint a representative of agricultural interests. He could also appoint a representative of a local or regional council (the governmental form for clusters of agricultural settlements). Thus the selection of a non-agricultural interest group would not necessarily be guaranteed.

CPAL membership consists of two representatives from the Ministry of Interior, two representatives from the Ministry of Agriculture, one representative each from the Ministry of Housing and Defense, and one representative from the settlement organizations appointed by the Ministry of Interior on the basis of a recommendation of the Jewish Agency (itself a settlement organization). Additionally, there is a representative of the national planning organization, one from local government, and two agricultural representatives appointed by the Minister of Interior. The Minister also appoints the chairman. Two facts stand out: The potential for rural dominance is clear, and the Ministry of Interior has a key role. The CPAL, which helps the ministry to regulate land-use nationally, has been statutorily assigned a narrow area of responsibility — the preservation of agricultural land. But the nature of this responsibility, in terms of authority over land use, gives it a powerful planning policy role.

## Rule-Making as Structural Policy

Rules are designed to eliminate conflict by providing an authoritative frame of reference. To operate by rules an organization must (1) be committed to act according to them, and (2) expect formal and informal sanctions when one deviates from them. When a rule-making agency is also invested with final decision-making authority — as is the CPAL — there is likely to emerge strong pressure on the agency, and confrontation involvement.

The CPAL is consistently pressured to alter land-use designations and to assume a role beyond mere rule making for agriculture use. The organization itself would prefer the limited role as outlined in the 1965 PBL (i.e., they would prefer to designate land rather than become involved in the larger planning questions). The CPAL is brought into an inevitable political role when it interacts with the numerous planning actors — developers, planners, local and central government agencies — and when it (frequently) assumes a more active role than vetoing or releasing agricultural land for urban use. It actually licences urban uses, acts as a watch-dog and hears appeals. The CPAL, then, has a dual role: to preserve agricultural land, on the one hand, and to assume a broad planning view (and the concomitant recognition of the need for releasing agricultural land for urban purposes), on the other hand. The CPAL sets (or changes) procedure, which allows it to exercise veto, approval or licensing decisions. This is a systemic phenomenon related to the stages of development of the organization and to the political culture. The aim is to achieve primacy.

An example of the use of procedure by the CPAL is to be found in an early effort to bypass the statutorily provided Board of Appeal (consisting of five members of the NPBC) over CPAL decisions. The proposal was that to appeal a CPAL decision, the plaintiff should come before the full CPAL. The proposal would have been parallel to, but would somewhat negate, existing procedure. It would have introduced difficulties for applicants and set the stage for an extended bargaining process even before the use of the final statutorily provided appeal. This appeal procedure was to be the setting for the case-by-case approach, which was eventually adopted as the general policy of the CPAL. Repeated discussion is an invitation for politics to replace general procedure, and would leave power of decision in the hands of the CPAL. The political implications of repeated discussion were clear to all, but this solution was deemed preferable to outside appeals in the NPBC.

## Institutionalizing Land-Use Procedures

How, then, did the CPAL go about setting up its decision procedure? Shortly after its establishment in 1965, the CPAL proceeded to form the framework for its structural policy by mapping the country in order to distinguish agricultural land from non-agricultural uses. Prior to 1965 it was possible for a developer, in cooperation with a local government, to infringe on the rule of non-building on cultivated land by drawing attention to the unclear status of certain lands. The mapping of the country meant that all development projects would have to come before the CPAL to seek a decision on allocation.

In 1968, the CPAL considered a report of a special commission of experts which proposed a classification of agricultural land in the country. The government appointed, and CPAL supported, a commission which consisted of representatives of the Center for Agricultural Planning, the Ministry of Interior, the Land Management Authority (LMA), and the Ministry of Agriculture. The absence of urban representation is glaring. The reason behind this unbalanced make-up is that, in general, urban interests are less articulated or politically aggregated. The Ministry of Interior is their closest defender. The planners, who represent the Ministry of Interior on the CPAL, are likely to be influenced by the organizational dynamics in the CPAL. They tend to view the CPAL as a means of influencing urban planning. But they do not represent urban interests directly as does the Ministry of Agriculture for rural interests.

It is instructive to discuss the experts' report in that it explicates the process and basis for the delineation of the CPAL structural policy, the confrontation that took place within the CPAL, and how rules concerning the release of agricultural land for urban use evolved. The report listed all open space in 75 jurisdictions as agricultural. Not all the communities were considered, because the remaining areas were outright cultivated agricultural lands. The major issue was the "delineation of agricultural areas within city limits...."[7] This goal was put to an immediate test by Ministry of Interior planners who wanted to know how the committee would handle the L-Plan area in the city of Tel Aviv (the hotly debated agricultural land release for urban development planning issues in the 1960s is discussed in chapter 6). The policy was defined as follows: "Every area that is not built on is to be declared as agricultural"[8] — a policy that had an immense detrimental potential on urban development and planning in cities. A second challenge came from the Ministry of Housing. The planning system gives access to decision making in various organizations. The Ministry of Housing has direct access in the CPAL and is involved in urban planning and development. Since many major urban development projects and housing plans were designated in peripheral areas of the various urban jurisdictions on agricultural land, the ministry was interested in a decision that those development projects which actually began in agricultural areas would go on as before. It was an issue that lingered on and which the ministry eventually won with the qualification that plans that were in the process of preparation would have to be considered in the light of the experts' report; previously approved plans (in the LPBC and the RPBC) would not have to be considered. The CPAL also dealt with technical as well as substantive matters. For example, concern was expressed over future changes in the maps that were initially prepared for the experts' report.

However, questions of technicalities were soon replaced by assertions of sectorial, normative positions. The representative of the agricultural interests noted "that the experts' report had statutory power which made it difficult to change the designation of land (from agricultural to urban) [or] to reexamine plans that were already approved in the past [or] examine whether they are justified. The declaratory statutory power of the experts' report," he argued, "serves the law, and the declaration of the slate of agricultural lands should be approved. If there is an important plan, we should consider it again."[9] This was a most clear statement in favor of a structural policy that would strengthen the ability of the CPAL to be a key factor with regard to urban land-use policy.

The experts' report and the list of agricultural areas gained the support of the government ministries. Later, the entire list of agricultural areas was published as a binding statutory declaration in governmental bulletins. In this way a basic position received legal sanction. The declaration decision implied that all previously approved plans on agricultural land would be reconsidered by the CPAL. Specific rules were set and the framework for future appeals for change of land designations, based on the lists of designated agricultural areas as outlined by the experts' committee and approved by the CPAL, was set out. This policy decision negated previous rules and procedures. Making the experts' report a declaration with statutory power assured the CPAL that most open areas, even non-agricultural, were mapped and that all future plans would have to be submitted to them for final review and approval. Indeed, even areas of dunes and arid deserts, such as the Negev, which is not likely to be cultivated in the foreseeable future, was covered by the declaration of the expert's report.[10] The CPAL felt free to designate desert and dune areas as agricultural by declaring them to be potential water reserves. Future urban planning was affected by designating as agricultural the many empty tracts of land in urban places, some of which were already designated in urban outline plans, although the plans might not necessarily have been yet approved by the LPBC or the RPBC.

## Urban Interests

Any new policy proposal generates conflict because it activates forces of opposition. But it is not always easy to determine who is affected by a policy, or what resources might be activated. Land-use policy generates political involvement from a variety of interests, which may include opposition by (outside) private interests, and opposition by organizations with formal access to the decision-making body. As the opposition attempts to alter policy decisions, so the CPAL re-establishes its structural policy elements that were attached. Following the publication of the statutory declaration about agricultural land designation there was much criticism in the press, and various potentially affected groups and organizations sought changes. It was clear to all that an important structural policy anchored in a statutory declaration and in the 1965 PBL would affect planning policy and was likely to further hinder urban and housing development, which could take place in the only reserve land available — agricultural land. The opposition varied from private groups to a government ministry. The next step is to consider how the CPAL dealt with this confrontation in their dealings with the various interested parties.

The CPAL attempted to reassert its newly acquired roles and position. Members realized that if they could overcome the opposition their organization would have *the* key role in planning. One of the first proposals to combat the opposition was made by the Ministry of Interior representative. In response to public criticism, the tactic he suggested was to urge the CPAL to simply accept the experts' report, and its publication in the official government bulletin, *Rishumot*, as a statutory declaration. The Ministry of Interior assessed the public criticism and overruled its appointee on the CPAL, who fully identified with his CPAL role. The ministry attempted to calm public criticism, not to confront it head on.

On April 15, 1968, it announced that the two-year period prescribed by the 1965 PBL, during which the CPAL had to designate all land which it deemed agricultural, was extended. This meant that the CPAL would have to exercise a case-by-case approach, instead of a general policy approach whereby, according to its declaration, all unbuilt land would be considered as agricultural. Because it was impossible for the CPAL to work on a plot-by-plot basis, it was unlikely that it could prevent all urban construction during the transitional period. This undefined situation also helped overcome the problem of the already approved plans and plans in preparation.

The Ministry of Interior representative acted in this matter from the organizational perspective of the CPAL. This commitment to the CPAL, in competition with the parent organization, reflects an actor's identification with the norms dominant in the immediate organization. The exhibited conflict of loyalties also resulted from the fact that the representative of the Ministry of Interior was a professional planner who perhaps saw in the CPAL an opportunity to exercise control over planning which was not at the time available in the ministry. He viewed the publication of the experts' report as a compelling declaration which would assure that the local (and especially regional) planning commissions submit for review all plans in the agriculturally declared areas. The strategy was to establish the review power and veto right of the CPAL at all levels of planning: "We shall consider all plans. There will clearly be some plans that will be released for development and construction, but it is clear that we shall prove our position regarding each case."[11] The planners of the Ministry of Interior were allied with and supported by the representatives of the agricultural and settlement organizations. The Ministry of Interior, which fenced off opposition by extending the time period required to designate all land, looked with favor on any strengthening of its role in urban planning and thus ended up supporting the CPAL position (and that of its chief planner representative). The ministry then waited for further developments in order to assess the strength of the opposition to this policy position. The agricultural representatives on the CPAL were also in favor. The challenge to this planning policy of strict review by the CPAL came from the Ministry of Housing, the public, the press, and various private organizations.

## Interest and Pressure Group Opposition

The publication of the experts' report, and its support by the CPAL via the declaration of all non-built land as agricultural, brought a number of urban interest groups into the scene. Before discussing the most important of these it is pertinent to ask whether the pressure of interest group opposition to a policy can be effective? It is beyond the scope of the present discussion to consider interest group politics in Israel, but in analyzing the opposition to this particular planning policy, the proposition made here and in other planning policy contexts is that access to decision centers enables effective opposition by different means such as coalitions and alliances, which are usually more effective than other avenues of access. Thus a private group that has no formal access, or does not represent an organization which figures in the national power distribution arrangements (such as a government coalition or party faction), is not likely to effectively oppose policy.

A. Guzman, Chairman of the Association of Landowners (AL), an established and recognized urban interest group and lobby, led the confrontation against the CPAL's rule-making and structural policy. Guzman demanded that the CPAL give up the review power over ongoing plans or plans in preparation, and change the sweeping declaration of all non-built land as agricultural. Guzman threatened *deus ex machina* action (a typical response in Israel's political culture). He referred to the ability of his lobby group to communicate with powerful government organizations, and reminded the CPAL that already in 1964 his association negotiated directly with the Ministry of Finance to remove the local tax on land, leaving in force only a national tax.

In Israel, access to the highest authority of government for various interest groups is relatively easy. Such access gives further support to the contention that policy outputs in Israel's political system are determined through the generation of inter-organizational conflict within the government. One of the strategies used by the AL was to point to a particular concern of the government, namely that many diaspora Jews have invested in land in Israel, and they might be adversely affected by the declaration on agricultural land. Guzman argued that the AL was instrumental in bringing Jewish investors from abroad into the land and property market in Israel, and claimed that this was done under instructions from the Ministry of Finance. The declaration, so the argument ran, had the potential effect of lowering prices and had an adverse effect on the land market. The activation of resources is an important element in such situations. When the association realized the ramifications of the statutory declaration concerning agricultural land they reported that they secured promises from the Prime Minister and Ministry of Finance that the declaration would be modified.[12]

The AL demanded that the declaration be cancelled because it caused a change in the designation of lands already planned for development, but on which so far there had been no construction. Given the CPAL's own spot-by-spot approach, it was suggested that the whole issue of agricultural land in urban centers be reconsidered, so that urban considerations (existing plans of development, cost, etc.) could be taken into account. The demand to consider urban development was, of course, opposite to the position held by the CPAL. Their position was to preserve land for agriculture and, alternatively, to release land only under its power of review. Only in this way would they control urban growth.

The confrontation with the Association of Landowners highlighted the CPAL's power of veto. The conflict situation explored how and with what resources one could confront a strong veto and benefit public organization. In the confrontation that took place with the AL, it was not concepts of distributive justice that were salient, but the political organization of the distribution of power and the regulation of important national goals. Because the declaration on agricultural land emanated in great part from one sectorial interest (agricultural), the reference by the AL to general national preferences and sensitivities (e.g., to Jewish investments from abroad), and the threat of appeal to a higher organization, could conceivably be effective and lead to overcoming the sectorial interest.

Thus, the issue before the CPAL was twofold: to retain the review power over the use of land acquired through the statutory declaration, and to assure organizations with a stake in urban planning that it was flexible enough to recognize needs of urban development. The essential issue was to avoid a major confrontation, which might activate higher governmental organizations that could possibly force a change in the structural policy and rule-making privileges acquired under the statutory declaration. The opposition of the private interest group in itself could be overcome, but together with opposition from other organizations such as the Ministry of Housing, it posed a serious threat to the CPAL.

## Opposition by Systemic Interests

Systemic opposition refers to those interests that have a formally assigned access in the CPAL and elsewhere in the power distribution network. This opposition is likely to involve powerful organizations, such as the Ministries of Housing, Transportation, Justice and Labor, which have access to and can penetrate planning decision centers. For example, the negative implications of the declaration as far as urban development and housing plans were concerned were expressed by the Ministry of Housing's representative on the CPAL: "My ministry has an interest in the matter. According to the declaration, all the work of the Ministry of Housing will be made nil. We will have to evolve plans for approval in this CPAL committee. We oppose the declaration only in those matters that concern our plans."[13] The opposition took the form that (1) plans that were already approved by the LPBC and RPBC would remain so, and that (2) all plans and site selection agreements with the Land Management Authority (LMA), some of which were already approved even in the CPAL, would be excluded from the rules of the declaration. The representative of the Ministry of Housing, like the representative of the AL, also raised the argument of the adverse effect that the declaration would have on overseas Jewish investment in real estate in Israel.

Although the position of the Ministry of Housing in planning decision arenas is obviously potentially far more effective than that of any private group (such as the AL), similar policy positions are discernable. Like the AL, the ministry viewed itself as an urban entrepreneur ready to oppose and enter into confrontation with "public" planning organizations such as the CPAL. The multiplicity of roles of the ministry enable it to fight for its goals and survival under favorable systemic conditions: access, heavy resources, and mutual dependencies with other government ministries.

The representative of the Ministry of Housing on the CPAL was able to alert his organization to the new policy as outlined in the declaration. In referring to a higher authority, the ministry noted that the plans under consideration were part of the government's housing policy. The presented data showed that 70 percent of the already approved plans of the ministry was on land which had previously been released from agricultural designation, but which was now, following the declaration, returned to agricultural status. If, therefore, the declaration was to be followed, the ministry would have to immediately halt all construction and terminate contracts. And this would create unemployment.[14]

## Interministerial Competition

To retain its dominance in planning policy decisions, the Ministry of Interior would have to confront the Ministry of Housing, retain the declaration, but yet offer a solution to the problem of the ongoing plans. The Ministry of Interior was set on having the CPAL retain the power to act under the declaration. It reiterated, via an opinion of its legal advisors, that the CPAL was mandated to reconsider each case and spot separately, and to reassess each of the previously approved plans. Acceptance of this opinion would strengthen the CPAL's role as a veto and benefit organization. The Ministry of Housing's efforts for a block release of all its ongoing and planned projects from the declaration countered the CPAL's policy position to have each project reviewed. The issue really revolved around the power of review of the CPAL, and not legal interpretations. The CPAL and the Ministry of Interior adhered to its legal position, and the CPAL continued in its efforts to retain its power to review specific plans. The Ministry of Housing countered this stance by using system breakdown arguments. The ministry argued that stoppage of work was bound to take place because local governments could not, after the declaration, issue permits for construction, even for lands that had received approval through all the planning organizations. The ministry was prepared for a confrontation with the Ministry of Interior, and especially with the CPAL.

However, the CPAL was not ready for a confrontation over a new policy against a variety of powerful actors. The political resolution of the conflict involved an admission by the CPAL that stoppage of work was inconceivable, but they nevertheless reiterated that it was not possible to provide specific automatic release of previously approved and ongoing plans. The agreed solution was that the Ministry of Housing provide a list of the developments they felt should be released from the statutory declaration, and that the CPAL would look favorably on the requests. In order to avoid confrontation, which would obviously involve an appeal to a higher authority and threaten the primacy of the CPAL and its power of review, the Ministry of Interior agreed to this solution. Its representative argued that it was possible, on a case-by-case basis,

for the CPAL to release Ministry of Housing plans from the jurisdiction of the declaration without losing the power of review. Conflict resolution was also aided by the continuous interdependence
of the two ministries which, in various planning policy issues,
preferred to use opportunities to cooperate and compromise.

Those CPAL members who did not represent governmental
ministries continued to fight against any deviation from the primacy position, even though they knew that such a policy would
lead to severe conflict. Those from the agricultural organizations
recalled the strong position of the Ministry of Housing, and related that previously the ministry and the Land Management
Authority "did what they pleased" (i.e., designated areas for development and construction and went ahead with their plans irrespective of other organizations). They cited examples of the ministry's infringement on agricultural interests. A typical position
was as follows: "There are a hundred acres of agricultural land
which the kibbutzim are cultivating — we cannot release the territory for construction just because the Ministry of Housing wants
it to be released from agricultural to construction land."[15] "The
CPAL should guard agricultural land, check each plan of the
Ministry of Housing, and perhaps save some acres of agricultural
land."[16] Their position was clearcut: to protect agricultural interests and locations. To achieve this, a general regulative concept
was required — hence the insistence of some CPAL members on a
structural policy that set rules and guidelines for each specific request. They opposed the automatic release from the agricultural
status of areas that were planned for urban development and
which had already been approved by the planning organizations.

One of the issues raised by the Ministry of Housing was that
the CPAL should have checked all plans before the statutory
declaration was decided on. In this way, it was argued, they would
not have "surprised" such a sizeable builder as the Ministry of
Housing. The CPAL was clearly set on increasing and institutionalizing its power of review, in gaining recognition for the experts' report and the statutory declaration, and in generally promoting the structural policy that would give it the capacity to consider each plan separately. Had the CPAL consulted other organizations prior to the issuance of the declaration, it would have faced
conflicts that it could not conceivably have won. Each major actor
would have claimed the right to become involved. The relative secrecy of the adoption of the experts' report gave it the desired edge
over others who had to come to it as supplicants — an altogether

different mode than participating in formulating a policy. The role identification of some of the representatives of the government ministries with the CPAL further contributed to this strategy.

The CPAL was set on retaining its power to review plans by playing a key role in conflict resolution. It solved one conflict with the Ministry of Housing through a questionable compromise. It would also manage the confrontation between the diehard agriculturalists and the Ministry of Housing by generating interministerial agreement. A new interpretation argued that only the land where the ministry is actually building should be released from the declaration by the CPAL. This position was also supported by the Ministry of Agriculture. With this growing coalition it became relatively easy to formally require the Ministry of Housing to submit a list of land tracts and parcelled areas that were previously approved for construction.

In retaining its power of review of urban plans, the decision processes within the CPAL and between ministries reflected specific policy positions. Member representatives of ministries often deviated from what was their home organizational position; in the critical stages they either convinced their organization or represented it. The next section considers the statutory declarations of land as agriculture. It provides a useful basis for understanding the CPAL's decisions and its normative bases, and the concomitant implications for urban planning.

## Policy Institutionalization vs. Group Interests

To retain control over its right to determine its own structural policy would establish the CPAL's power of review over urban development; it would affect land use planning and establish the CPAL as a veto and benefit allocating planning organization. This required conflict resolution, which itself involved accommodation of the planning and building needs of strong actors. The alternative would have involved major conflicts over the basic roles of the CPAL in planning. The process of accommodation would be likely to enhance the efforts to institutionalize rules and thus it involved elements of exchange. To the Ministry of Interior and the CPAL it was of major importance to have the power to review specific spots accepted. Its corollary would be a measure of institutionalization of strict rules on the release of land. The political response by the Ministry of Housing and by the AL urban pressure group was to threaten to appeal to a higher authority.

The CPAL knew that an appeal to a higher authority would exacerbate the conflict. It had no way to predict its outcome. The CPAL's concern was for survival, and thus they compromised in order to protect their main goal — which was the institutionalization of land-use planning procedure. One position was that urban land would be freed from the declaration, while the oppositionists recognized the CPAL's review authority regarding the project-by-project approach. To remove open urban land from the review power could have removed the CPAL from urban decisions. The CPAL preferred to issue a general rule regarding the release of planned and ongoing projects, while maintaining control through the project-by-project review approach. Lowi commented that "avoidance of rule making is more of a usurpation than rule making [itself]." Indeed, the absence of rules is likely to create an irresponsible political process.[17] The CPAL wanted the power of review, which would create a bargaining situation for each case, but under institutionalized rules.

In contrast to the policy of releasing open and agricultural land in urban areas for development, the AL wanted a more general policy, which would release from the statutory declaration all open space in urban areas and not specifically land (or projects) under planning or intended for development and housing. The aim of the urban group was to free all land in urban areas from the clutches of the agricultural interests. Indeed, it made little planning sense for areas adjacent to the city of Tel Aviv, such as the L-Plan area, to be under agricultural designation and hence under the power of review of agricultural interests (see chapter 6). However, given the major reform of planning policy structures, procedures and contents generated by the 1965 PBL, the CPAL as an organization involved in land-use policy could not but continue to fight for its power to review. When major structural policy changes occur in a political system, and organizations such as the CPAL are in search of a role, interest groups find it difficult to succeed when radical planning policy conflicts are involved. Yet, it is exactly when new policies emerge on the public agenda that interest groups rise to action.

Had the urban interest group achieved their main demand for a sweeping release of land, it would have lessened considerably the CPAL's role in urban planning. However, they did not achieve their aim, and this hardened the policy position of interested parties. For example, the Ministry of Agriculture refocused the issue to make sure that the CPAL had not only power of review but also power of veto, which would establish the CPAL's benefit allocation role. "Our role is to release lands from the agricultural status for construction. If there is in a city plan an area that is designated as agricultural and a city engineer (planner) determines that it ought to be developed and built on, this is brought before the CPAL."[18] The adopted strategy was that release from the statutory declaration was not negotiable; the declaration was viewed as a fact. "We guard agricultural land, so that it is not wasted. There cannot be automatic release of land from agricultural status. In each case there must be an appeal to the CPAL, and the committee will consider each request."[19] No policy and decision body could state more clearly its opposition to deal with urban issues on the basis of general principles.

The CPAL's confrontation with the urban interests of the AL brought forth a key resource at their disposal. Opponents to the CPAL challenged the techniques by which the experts' report was prepared. Success here would be a major challenge to the CPAL's structural policy. When the chairman of the experts' committee explained how they classified the land, it immediately became apparent that the committee intended to increase the power of the CPAL. The chairman first stated that the committee intended to examine, community by community, which agricultural land was already designated for construction and development, and to bring the issue of the land's status before the Ministry of Interior for an opinion. But the CPAL's committee of experts discarded this procedure because of a legal deadline it faced. Had the committee not declared that all land which had no actual construction or development on it was agricultural land, many of the plans approved by the planning hierarchy (but not by the CPAL) for construction and development would have taken effect two years after approval. The chairman explained that his committee of experts decided "to do their jobs so that the CPAL would be able to be the final determiner of what should be released from agricultural designation." It was decided by the experts' committee that "any area that is not built on or developed would have to be reexamined by the CPAL which could then decide on corrective action."[20]

The experts' report served the CPAL well in that it gave the organization jurisdiction over all open land, including land for which there were development and construction plans and which were previously approved by the planning organizations. The mode of preparation and the mapping of land left little doubt that it proceeded from a preconceived notion that the CPAL should and would be at the center of all urban land-use policy decisions in agriculturally designated land.

## Institutionalizing Rules by Accommodation

The experts' report could have been challenged on both technical and substantive grounds. The problem for the CPAL was how to retain its position, to have all cases brought before it for review, to assure that no changes were made in the statutory declaration concerning the agricultural lands, and at the same time to satisfy the opposition so that no change would be imposed from above. The CPAL devised a strategy to overcome opposition which included a variety of accommodating measures. The policy of assert and accommodate prevented the appeal to a higher authority and kept all demands within the immediate controlled conflict arena of the CPAL. It was aided in this by the short range policy goals of the urban interest groups and other interest organizations. Thus, the CPAL told the AL that they would remove from the declaration the clauses concerning small plots owned by individuals. This group had the potential to elicit public and political empathy and generate action against the declaration. The CPAL strategy was aimed at the constituency of the AL, rather than at the Association's representatives. The Ministry of Agriculture, in asserting the importance of the statutory declaration as a tool for the CPAL to retain the hold over land, suggested that they remove from the declaration only those areas that were clearly for construction and development — not necessarily all approved plans of construction: "This was intended to show flexibility, but mostly it would show that we are doing our best for the release of land from the statutory declaration and that we are not unbending in our consideration."[21] The Ministry of Interior wanted the CPAL to retain control and to overcome the opposition to the experts' report. Their representative adopted the stance that the CPAL should reconsider approved plans for construction, but only in areas of dunes, desert and arid land. The proposal left out the vast areas of cultivated and semi-cultivated land in urban centers. This measure of flexibility by the ministry could hardly been expected to satisfy either the Ministry of Housing or the Association of Landowners. The CPAL tried delaying tactics. It suggested that a study be undertaken to ascertain exactly which lands should be released from the declaration. Furthermore, a request was made to Mr. Guzman, head of the AL, to provide a list of plans which he wished to be released from the agricultural statutes. It was argued in the CPAL that "the preparation of such a list will take them much time, and this might lessen their arguments against us."[22]

Minor accommodations and delaying tactics were important in order to gauge the extent of the threat of appeal to a higher authority, which would have endangered the CPAL in its current vulnerable institutionalization efforts. The issue was whether the Ministry of Housing and the AL had enough leverage with the Treasury or the Prime Minister in their attempt to alter the experts' report, the statutory declaration, or the decisions of the CPAL regarding plans in progress or approved plans.

In this context a generalization can be made about Israel's politics of policy arenas. There is a low commitment to a general policy; ad hoc policy decisions are common, especially when they enable the calming of agitation, which, when accommodated on an *ad hoc* basis, allow continued dominance. The CPAL, because it is a statutory body, could have opted for a strategy of opposing or even ignoring interference from above; but higher authorities have access to the appointment of CPAL members and to the appeal board of the CPAL — the National Planning and Building Council (NPBC). Thus the CPAL opted for a strategy of having mutually agreed estates of action. This is a model organizational pattern in the Israeli policy process which usually mellows the various organizations involved in a conflict and avoids head-on clashes. The concern over possible government reaction was real. Members of the CPAL realized the potential capacity of the government to change the structural policy that gave the CPAL such power over the rules of the game. To assure that a clash with the government was not in the making, the planner from the Ministry of Interior had urgent talks with the Treasury. Later he was able to report back to the CPAL that the Treasury agreed with the CPAL general policy position that no general release from the declaration should be made. Armed with information that interference from above was not forthcoming, the CPAL was free to make its decisions on how to handle both the Ministry of Housing and the AL.

The decision of the CPAL reflected its efforts to institutionalize (1) the experts' report intact, so that all rule making regarding the release of agricultural land would emanate from it and from case-by-case decisions; (2) its role as a benefit allocator; (3) its veto role; and (4) its central role in urban planning. Specifically, it decided that the plans for housing and development that were already approved or were in the process of approval would be given priority consideration. No automatic release of these plans would be given. Furthermore, the above mentioned delaying proposal — requesting the AL to submit a list of land and plans which they wanted to release from the declaration — was accepted. The only deviation was in favor of the Ministry of Housing. It was decided that the ministry would continue its negotiations with the CPAL over lands and housing which the ministry wanted released from the declaration. In this way a major organization was excluded from CPAL decisions.

The CPAL reached consensus on the need to guard agricultural land and release land that could not be cultivated, retained its capacity to review all plans (including those that were already approved), to approve changes of land designation as mandated by the experts' report, and to review each plan for possible conflicts with already existing approvals. In sum, each approved plan would have to go before the CPAL for consideration.

The CPAL decided to go public presumably in order to assert its newly institutionalized role and to show flexibility over questions of urban development matters. A press release revealed a most minimal exclusion from the general policy. It noted that approved development plans on dune sand and arid areas were to be automatically released from the declaration. This, according to the CPAL, "will calm the agitated spirits and will enable individuals to appeal to the committee for approval."[23]

No participatory forum was acceptable to the CPAL. Members vehemently opposed a proposal that the CPAL appoint an advisory regional commission, whose role would be to recommend, with regard to approved plans, the removal of those lands from the rules of the declaration. Membership of the commission was expected to include the participation of a representative of the Regional Planning and Building Commission (RPBL), the local governments concerned, and a public representative (such as from the AL). The aim of the CPAL was to keep the power of review over each application. Another rationale against the regional advisory boards reflected the CPAL's view that it represented the public interest against sectorial interests. The rejection of regional participation from decision making was due to the fact that the Ministry of Interior was designated as the forum to reconsider plans and make recommendations to the CPAL. The Ministry of Interior, aided by its representative on the CPAL, seized on the controversial issue as an opportunity to assume a further role. In this way the ministry further institutionalized itself in urban planning policy: it emerged with the responsibility to prepare the review of plans and appeals. The implementation would be in the planning section of the Ministry of Interior, which has two members on the CPAL, directly appoints three more members, and chairs the forum. The result was that it increased the influence of the ministry in determining planning policy outcomes.

We have dealt at some length with the structural policy set by the CPAL. The CPAL operates on the basis of the mapping of the country and institutionalizing rules of review of plans. Plans come before it for review; it then exercises the key role that it evolved for itself. The assigned access and roles to different organizations concerned with planning enabled the Ministry of Housing, for example, to be involved in CPAL decisions and this affects the CPAL's political behavior. Political involvement and influence in planning is more readily available to systemically assigned organizations (such as the Ministry of Housing) than for private interest organizations.

The power to set rules concerning the designation of land gives the CPAL the ability to advance norms in the planning process and become dominant in urban planning. In doing so it often generates further conflict. The following section concentrates on the political involvement of the CPAL in local planning (i.e., how the institutional interests of the CPAL vs. local community interests clash, and how they are resolved in a series of accommodations, alliances and legal confrontations).

## Local Initiatives in a National Setting

We can assess the challenge to the institutionalization efforts of rule making and relative power by the CPAL in how this review body handles the actual urban and planning policy politics of local communities. Community confrontation with the CPAL involves the system of planning: the local, regional and national planning and building commissions — the LPBC, RPBC and NPBC, respectively. Governmental agencies and party leaders usually become part of ephemeral alliances with these bodies, and have to interact in relation to the CPAL's institutionalized

119

structural policy and systemically prescribed planning role. In order to understand how planning works in Israel, actual knowledge of how interactions on the local level take place is essential.

Local communities mobilize support for their particular plans in the regional commission by gaining the support of a variety of organizations outside the planning hierarchy. When a local community takes on the CPAL it has to overcome the veto power which the review body is only too ready to exercise. Being sectorially structured, urban communities are not likely to find too many potential allies in the CPAL. Whereas in the RPBC one finds a similar representation of the government political coalition, in the CPAL it is more one-sided. The RPBC, or the Ministries of Housing or Interior, may want to accommodate an urban community, but they can be blocked by the CPAL. A community may also appeal to the Supreme Court. A common pattern is for a community to appeal to one organization in order to influence the other, and to create conditions for a change of decision. For example, a community may use the planning staff of the regional commission to persuade the CPAL on planning grounds to release land from agricultural designation, or appeal to the CPAL for a release so that the RPBC may decide on the community's request (free of the agricultural designation veto). Both the CPAL and the RPBC are likely to face government or party leaders who ally with the community. The major difficulty in interacting with the CPAL is the need to overcome a normative position anchored in an organization capable of issuing an authoritative veto.

In this section we briefly explicate on: (1) the potential veto and benefit allocation roles available to the CPAL in local planning; (2) the linkage point that it provides between the local and regional planning commissions and the local community; and (3) the types of appeals (including judicial ones) and resources used in interactions between the CPAL and local communities. In this process of implementation the CPAL's structural policy will be tested. We ask whether the rules are sufficiently institutionalized to prevent disruptive confrontations and bargaining? We expect the structural policy to be scrutinized by those affected by it in the communities. Social pressures rather than agricultural considerations are likely to be the major determinants of the benefit allocation role of the CPAL. This is illustrated in the development efforts of Yad, a not-well-to-do community on the outskirts of Tel Aviv. Yad wanted to ease its severe housing problems and requested a change in the agricultural designation of 20 acres, and an annexation of 90 acres. Prior to Yad's application, the wealthy neighboring community of Sam had submitted to its local planning commission its own housing plan for the same 20 acres.[24] The local planning commission (Sharon South), which has jurisdiction over the area, requested that the CPAL provide guidelines concerning the release of this land.[25] Yad's request was made to the Minister of Interior, who established an ad-hoc committee to consider the request of the annexation of a municipal area without municipal status, which was Yad's position.

The CPAL decided to approve the transfer of 20 acres to Yad because of its pressing need for low cost public housing,[26] and not to approve the Sam request. Moreover, the ruling stipulated that at least 250 housing units were to be built for needy young couples. Thus, not only did the CPAL deviate from the strict preservation of agricultural land approach, but it also intervened in the planning goals of a local community. The CPAL also reserved for itself the right to review and approve Yad's detailed plan, following its approval by the local and regional planning commissions. In this way the CPAL intended to supervise the specific use of the land.

Sam appealed to the Supreme Court to reject the CPAL's transfer of land to Yad. The Supreme Court interpreted the role of the CPAL narrowly and on the basis of the original intent rather than on the evolved CPAL policy. The court stated: "The [CPAL] will not use its authority except when needed for the preservation of agricultural land and its agricultural use."[27] The CPAL's role in regard to Yad's distressing social problems were laudable, the court argued, but not relevant to the CPAL's decision. The CPAL was not necessarily unhappy with the negation, since its involvement in community affairs had been caused by community and government ministerial pressure.

The Supreme Court referred to the internal proceedings of the CPAL, and pointed out that the CPAL had not withstood political pressure. One member said that he would have opposed the change of designation, but "we have no reason to expect that the government would uphold our decision. On the basis of lawful agricultural considerations, I would not approve. But, considering the external factors in this case, and in spite of the legal provisions, I give my consent...." Another member said: "I would oppose the transfer of land but I am aware of the pressures [exerted on the CPAL]...."[28] The chairman of the CPAL claimed that many pressures were being exerted. He stated: "The Minister of the Interior must now appear before the Knesset's Labor Affairs Committee and explain the reasons for which the CPAL does not comply with demands to release agricultural land for construction."[29] The pressures to which members of the CPAL referred, and which the Supreme Court quoted, were well known. At the time, a social reform group held street demonstrations for cheaper housing, especially for young, newly-wed couples. Their demands for improved living conditions for people of Eastern origin, whose relative socioeconomic status was low, focused attention on an emerging ethnic cleavage in Israel.

In responding to various pressures the CPAL decided not to resort to its veto power. Thus, in the light of social pressures, the CPAL's major source of weakness was exposed: the lack of a public land allocation policy for urban development. But because the CPAL decided to respond on an ad-hoc basis it avoided a major reform which it should have undertaken. In order to retain its dominance and power, it adopted a flexible mode of action. Urban development and sprawl required agricultural land. But Supreme Court decisions did not provide the needed perspective on urban development. It merely accentuated the CPAL's lack of a solid urban policy in view of growing social needs, bargaining, and the influence of the free market and individual choice. The Supreme Court's appeal decision, although based on the 1965 PBL, supported Sam's fear of proximity of low income housing. The Court declared: "In acquiescing to external pressure and in considering housing and development needs...as its responsibility, the CPAL has broken the dictates of the law. Not only did it deviate from its authority, but it also abandoned its duties as prescribed by law."[30] The earlier Supreme Court decision underscored the CPAL as a conservative force whose response to social urban needs is slow. In evolving its structural policy and in resolving conflict with urban and systemic interests, the CPAL's conflict resolution decisions went far ahead of what the above Supreme Court decision prescribed for urban development.

## Urban Developers vs. the CPAL

The CPAL's lack of an urban development policy can be further illustrated in another instance of Supreme Court intervention. In contrast to the preceding case, in this instance it was recognized that urban development needs were a legitimate part of the CPAL's decision arena.

A particular land-use plan was approved by the local and regional planning commissions prior to the declaration of land as agricultural by the CPAL. Nevertheless, when the CPAL decided to cancel the approval on the basis of the 1965 PBL, a construction company appealed to the Supreme Court. The appeal argued that planning and construction had already taken place in neighboring lots. In response, the Supreme Court supported a broad dual role for the CPAL. It referred to the privileges of the CPAL under the First Amendment, item 10, of the 1965 PBL, which gives the CPAL authority to designate land and even transfer land to agricultural status even when an approved plan allows urban construction. The Supreme Court noted this regulative power, but at the same time recognized that the CPAL has authority to consider urban development needs. In specific reference to the appealer, the Supreme Court noted that previous approval shows that the CPAL: "does not follow rigid policy lines...each case is considered by itself...the CPAL considers the situation as well as the need for new construction....The main task of the CPAL is preventing agricultural areas of the country from being swallowed up thoughtlessly and needlessly...by the urban mammoth which sends its arms in all directions and turns large areas into housing projects." The court also noted that the basis of the CPAL's activity is to balance agricultural and urban needs, and that this balancing function legitimizes the CPAL's judgments on urban development.[31] This remark by the court highlights the conflict of roles. The CPAL focused on its authority over non-built up urban land. In this particular instance a land-use plan was available. When the CPAL acts it opens the way to exercise a discretionary policy over community planning preference and planning development in general. The effort to institutionalize one policy (preservation of agricultural land) does not halt the search for other, even more contradictory roles in urban housing development and construction. The chairman of the CPAL welcomed the dual role and noted that "should the tendency to preserve agricultural land dominate planning issues, the road to development...would be blocked."[32] The Supreme Court's specific view of the development was that "Since there is much sandy and uncultivated land in our country...there is no justifiable reason for development to be undertaken on our relatively sparse agricultural areas." The Court recognized the priority of preserving agricultural land, and implicitly recognized the role of the CPAL over agricultural land which had urban development plans. It did not, however, completely ignore the dangers of wild deviations under political-economic pressure and therefore established that "a change in favor of urban development could take place, but only in unusual and essential cases...."[33]

The construction company had originally been able to secure the approval of both the statutory planning organizations and of the CPAL, which reviewed its plans. The change to agricultural status that the CPAL later demanded was reversed by the Supreme Court decision. But pressure politics also played a role. The LPBC and the RPBC, which represented local governments and the government (especially the Ministry of Interior), publicly supported the development. The intervention of the Supreme Court suggests that it recognized reasonable urban growth needs.

The above discussion highlights the CPAL's role in land-use planning through the use of its statutorily provided and evolved decision power, including the right of veto. While the case-by-case approach leaves the CPAL free to develop rules, exercise its veto power, and confer benefits to urban developers, it also leaves it open to appeals and to pressures. Had the CPAL a definite policy on urban development, or a release from agricultural designation policy, it would conceivably avoid many head-on conflicts with the various ministries and with private developers. However, because the case-by-case approach generally prevails, conflict is inevitable. The involvement of the CPAL in conflict bargaining stems from its preference for acting as both a rule-making veto and benefit allocating agency, and an appeal board for urban developers. It is inevitable that the CPAL would have a role in preserving agricultural land and in urban development. It considers each case separately, and since it has mapped the entire country and has designated most undeveloped and unbuilt areas as agricultural, urban development can only take place at the expense of agricultural land.

The rule-making, and veto and benefit allocating powers of the CPAL are in great part statutorily intrinsic but they express an evolutionary land-use planning policy. The CPAL is a power-wielding organization whose choice of behavior is determined by legal, social, economic and political factors. The Supreme Court implicitly recognized the dual role of the CPAL: to consider its preservation role as paramount, and to respond to urban needs only in special social circumstances. Various Supreme Court decisions have formalized that which the CPAL carries out in practice. The next step is to consider the ways by which CPAL powers come to bear on community development.

## Linkages Between Planning Organizations

When a local planning commission challenges a CPAL decision, it must find a way to overcome the veto power which the CPAL is only too ready to exercise. One way is to enlist the professional planning staff of the regional planning commission to persuade or appeal to the CPAL to release land from agricultural status. The major difficulty facing the LPBC involves overcoming a normative position which is institutionalized in an organization capable of issuing a veto. Since the CPAL membership primarily reflects agricultural interests, potential allies are not readily available in the CPAL. Even if a regional planning commission is ready to accommodate a local one, it can find itself blocked by the CPAL. If an alliance formed in the CPAL is in favor of a local community request, the RPBC can make a decision free of constraints. Local planning can thus be affected by the position of the regional planning commission, by the CPAL, or by both. Each of these organizations can become a linkage point, which serves as a leverage to influence the other. Often a community appeals to one organization in order to influence the other and to create conditions for a favorable decision.

A community has several options when planning the development of agricultural land situated within its jurisdiction. It may decide (1) to plan for non-agricultural development; (2) to plan it as a "green belt," open space or a park (if the area is not already being cultivated); or (3) to eliminate the area from its planning considerations. In each case it must submit the plan to the regional planning commission, where it is either rejected on planning or political grounds, or, if it is approved, forwarded to the CPAL for review. The CPAL can veto, approve, or modify the plan. When a RPBC favors a plan for non-agricultural development of agricultural land, it allies with the local community to argue the merits of the plan before the CPAL. Local community planning of development of agricultural land involves assessment of the chances of its release from agricultural status by the CPAL. It is likely to attempt and secure advance support from the regional planning body. Even prior to the professional and technical planning, building of support takes place, informal appeals are made, and political resources are activated. The linkages are illustrated graphically:

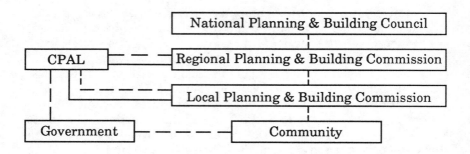

Solid lines show systemically and statutorily prescribed paths of influence; broken lines show paths of interaction.

A local community uses the RPBC as a linkage point to influence the CPAL (broken line) or it may use the CPAL as a linkage point in order to create favorable conditions for the review of its plan by the RPBC (solid line). In arguing before the CPAL, a local community attempts to gain acceptance for its planning interests. To succeed, it will design appeals involving social tensions and pressures on the community, and choose intermediary political resources — government and political party ones — to use in the interaction with the CPAL. Thus access for a community to decision-making organizations is available directly or indirectly.

In order to illustrate how linkage takes place we examined the linkages created by Run (a local community in the center of Israel), and the modes of appeals and resources used in its interactions.

## Local Government vs. the CPAL

Run, a relatively poor community, with a host of social problems, wanted to construct a football stadium on agricultural land that was sited within its jurisdiction. The problem was to have the

CPAL accept social and community reasons as a basis for stadium construction on agricultural land. The local council had decided to build the stadium following pressures by the Hapoel Sports Association (which is affiliated with the Histadrut Labor Federation) and by some of its members who were affiliated to the Labor party.

The local council first appealed to the Land Management Authority (LMA) requesting public land; ten, and later forty acres in close proximity to the local school were granted. (It is not uncommon for land to be allocated due to pressure by interest groups. Key figures, such as the Minister of Finance, can and often do intervene to facilitate the transfer of land to a community. It is often done to reward a loyal political ally or to alleviate social pressures or community tensions). The LMA allocation was to be used as a political resource before the CPAL. Prior to its appearance before the CPAL, the community prepared a plan for the stadium and secured the approval of the police on traffic matters. They also secured the support of the professional planning staff of the regional planning commission with whom they had regular contact. The local council felt confident that they would be granted permission, and even began to level the land. The RPBC then issued a stop order because the leveling was being carried out on agricultural land.

The case was presented to the CPAL by a member of the local council and its planner, who were later joined by the chairman of the council. Overlaping membership often brings unanticipated behavior. The LMA representative on the CPAL wanted to know why land was allotted before the CPAL was consulted. The organizational setting of the CPAL, and its normative features, were apparently stronger than the need to defend the parent organization (the LMA) and its position. The representative suggested that the local council find another location, pointing out that in this way the need for a change in land designation would be avoided. The local planner replied that within the physical jurisdiction of the local council, no area was large enough to accommodate a sports arena. Using his professional skills, the local planner provided elaborate topographical explanations of the structure of the land, water drainage patterns, etc., to show that the area requested was the only one suitable for the stadium. Moreover, he argued that a substantive element of the plan was an attempt to organize community involvement and to foster the identification of youth with their community.

The CPAL not only vetoed Run's request on the grounds of preserving agricultural land but also on the basis of local planning considerations. The representative of the Ministry of Interior on the CPAL argued, on purely planning grounds, that a number of football stadiums already existed in the area, and that another one was not needed. But he ignored, of course, the *raison d'etre* — namely community group competition. He suggested an alternative site, near a local seminary, so long as it would be within the existing plan and not on agricultural land. The local planner continued to provide procedural and substantive information, and noted that previous efforts to find a suitable location within the existing plans had not been successful. Furthermore, he argued, the area under discussion was agricultural only by designation: it was not being cultivated, nor was Run an agricultural community. Thus the retention of a few acres would only be of marginal importance to national agriculture, while its release would achieve an important impact on community cohesion.

But this argument proved to be an inappropriate strategy. Although CPAL members could not dispute the verity of the technical and social arguments, they did respond to what they regarded as interference in their sphere of influence. To veto they needed only fiat, not necessarily facts. In supporting the CPAL, an Agriculture Center representative (the strongest agricultural lobby in Israel) stated: "I am not aware of the details of plans for the region under consideration, but it is clear that there is a demand to change the designation of what will eventually amount to some 40 acres of agricultural land into a sports area. The obligation of this committee is to oppose this, including the four acres for the Hapoel Sports Association."[34] An RPBC planner recommended that the stadium be approved because of the pluralistic, ethnic nature of the community, which meant that it was necessary to have several sports facilities, and because development work had already begun.[35] Reference to financial investment obligations taken by the community confirmed that the local leadership had a deep commitment to the community issue and that it represented the authoritative political force. The idea of redundant services was basically accepted by the CPAL, but not on agricultural land. Faced with the demands of a socially unique community, election promises of key political figures, and the land allotment by the LMA, the CPAL was diverted and pressured to consider political contingencies rather than actual planning considerations. The CPAL faced a precedent situation. If one sports association received public agricultural land for a stadium, the CPAL would be unable to prevent others from obtaining the same.

The role of the Ministry of Interior as an overseer of local government led to it assuming a key role in the resolution of the conflict. Its representative informed the CPAL that, even though they were promised the agricultural land, the Hapoel Sports Association was willing to yield another tract that was in their possession. He suggested that this type of trade-off arrangement might be used in the future, and would retard an avalanche of requests. The CPAL wanted to prevent the current case from becoming a precedent. In order to do this the CPAL had to formally recognize and accommodate the role of community politics (the promise of rewards to various groups and the accompanying obligations these groups would undertake). The representative from the Ministry of Housing suggested that the small plot be approved for the Hapoel Sports Association, especially since it had already invested a significant amount of money for development, but that it should be made clear that no additional areas would be approved for other sports associations. It was a political attempt to hold the rope at both ends: on the one hand it was intended to preserve a great part of the agricultural land, and on the other hand to end the confrontation with representatives of a highly problematic community. Politics of compromise is very often considered and used by the CPAL in lieu of its veto power. Such outcomes are facilitated by the CPAL's case-by-case approach, which helps avert major confrontations by yielding when political pressures are too high.

Most CPAL members were determined to prevent the change in the agricultural designation of the land. But because of mounting pressures they were more concerned about retaining their role in planning. CPAL minutes indicate that they doubted their ability to defend the agricultural land preservation norm if it was challenged by governmental and political confrontation. This is evidenced by the elaborate planning argumentation of the CPAL. For example, it discussed expected traffic problems, a subject that was obviously not their concern, especially since the community had already secured police approval for the stadium's location. CPAL members also considered alternative sites and the number of stadiums needed in the community. Again, this interaction was not within its procedural or terms of reference. The CPAL's planning/political interactions reflected its basic desire to be a key factor in urban land-use planning. In the Run case it was motivated by a reluctance to have its procedural veto power jeopardized. The political nature of CPAL activities is further seen by the meager recourse to data and information during the entire confrontation with Run. The proposals the CPAL made about alternative sites, and the proposal to limit the land request to four acres, were not the result of a study or alternative planning. The proposals were made in the midst of bargaining. Only toward the end of the long negotiations was it revealed that the entire area planned for the stadium was being cultivated by a nearby kibbutz. This new information reactivated opposition by the Agricultural Center representative, who argued vehemently against any change in the agricultural designation. He warned, as he had before, that one concession would invite similar pressure for the remainder of the area, and "even logical alternatives will not be accepted then. Under pressure we shall have to approve all the area."[36] Making proposals of alternative sites, not on agricultural land, is certainly an indication of the CPAL's political role in planning. However, the Run local council fought against all alternative sites.

## Appeals and Political Resources

The type of appeals and resources used by the Run local community with the CPAL were not idiosyncratic, but representative of a common pattern in Israeli political culture. The interaction over substance and procedure is unique only so far as the issues involved are unique. The political pattern is consistently found in other planning situations involving the CPAL. The unstated policy of the CPAL is to deal with each unique situation while retaining dominance and regulating land use; the policy of any particular community is to find a politically legitimate way by which it can activate the benefit allocation role of the CPAL and overcome a veto or make it dormant. What type of appeals and resources are used in the process of a community's efforts to advance its planning goals? And how can they be effective, and under what conditions? Such questions are related not only to the particular conflict but also to whether the conflict (with an organization such as the CPAL) can be modified in some way.

Appeals to the CPAL likely to be made by a community can be based on: (1) altruism (approve the release of land because it is good for the community); (2) professional reasons (good community planning); (3) social reasons (the stadium is important for community well-being); (4) political reasons (approval is requested because the issue is related to community tensions, has the support of various political forces, and money was invested and commitments were made). Varied resources are used and allocated by a community in order to influence land-use decisions: (1) threat of appeal to higher level of authority; (2) mobilization of support (through support of regional planners, and ministerial support for allocation of public land); (3) political culture features (the threat of social unrest, political unrest); (4) use of a community structure (in the case of Run, the ethnic and family divisions of the community was introduced as a factor in requesting support for multiple sports arenas in a small community); and (5) illegal establishment of facts and reference to *de facto* expenditure and construction. While the above are not the only resources in planning interaction, they are representative. Support from political parties and their representatives in the government are related to yet another set of resources, involving increase in employment in the community and its future vote.

The key feature in the use of resources is the ability to use them not merely as a threat, but as part of the planning conflict, which involves appeal and exchange of resources (e.g., avoiding community unrest in exchange for the CPAL's favorable decision or a government minister's support). Resources can be tangible and intangible. They can be actually used or their use may only be threatened. Achieving goals is likely to result from some combination of use of the above, each case and situation having its unique mix.

The specific appeal and resources used (and exchanged) between Run and the CPAL were numerous. Following the professional appeal by the local planners, the chairman of the local council and the local worker's council, both known for their closeness to political party leaders and the Histadrut Labor Federation, became involved. They requested that the original plan for the sports center be approved and pointed to their ability to mobilize political support. They argued that the disputed agricultural area was given to Run by the LMA, for which they paid rent and were allowed by the LPBC to fence. The aid given to Run in planning by the regional planners was used as proof of the local planning processes as solid, professional planning. They implied that conflict would be intensified with the aid of national political organizations.[37] The local representative used threats of social unrest; he told the CPAL that the local Hapoel Sports

Association members wanted to demonstrate in front of CPAL offices, but that they had prevented them from doing so. They stressed that the community's hopes were high and that if disappointed, community unrest and social disorder would result.[38] In the history of Jewish settlement in Palestine, and later in Israel, the thrust of development has often preceded plans or permits. Interactions, appeals, alliances, parallel planning and action-oriented planning outputs have been valued (see chapter 6); procedure and legality have followed. Since the 1965 PBL, efforts were made by planning organizations to inculcate procedure into planning. The Run example shows the clash between the rooted attitude and efforts to emphasize planning procedures in substantive matters. The council repeatedly pointed to the heavy investment already made in the sports center. Whether the community of Run could deliver on all its threats and produce the alleged support it claimed to enjoy in higher political circles was not tested by the CPAL. The regulative body recognized that the community had resources which could be translated to influence and that a resolution to the conflict was in the best interest of its role as land-use regulator. The need to resolve conflict involves bargaining and compromise. The CPAL initiated discussions involving a possible future request for land. They wanted certain assurances, notably, that the community would not request agricultural land in the future. This would make it easier for the CPAL to approve the stadium. The major issue for the CPAL was that they would not be able to withstand future pressure from other sports associations. The CPAL, then, preferred to bargain than to exercise power. The CPAL's demand to the chairman of the local council never to request agricultural land in the future was an impossible one: the chairman of a local council must retain decision-making capabilities in order to prove that the local government can carry out its functions. Thus, the chairman proposed a position which argued that since the construction of the stadium had been already begun, and since the CPAL felt that there was no available space for additional stadiums, he would reject any future requests by other sports associations. This formulation left the local leaders with decision powers and assured the CPAL that its decision was indeed ad hoc and an exception, and was not indicative of its general policy on the release of land.

These political negotiations were based on the CPAL's principle of dealing with each case in lieu of a general policy on the release of land for urban use. The resolution of conflict reflected this and made it possible to treat Run's request as special and idiosyncratic. Once this was established the regional planner felt free to exercise his linkage position and argue as a professional. Jointly with the local council, a new outline plan, complete with alternatives, was prepared. Solutions for parking, and for an entrance from the main highway, were proposed. Furthermore, more acreage for the stadium was argued for: about five or six acres, which could include other community sports facilities. At the same time the regional planner supported the CPAL's view that any future request for sport facilities on agricultural land should not be heeded. Thus the regional planner adopted the conflict resolution position of both the local government and that of the CPAL.

The combined use of tangible and intangible resources resulted in CPAL approval of five acres for the Run stadium. The resources used by the community are identifiable. The CPAL, by taking the time to review Run's appeal, allowed the community to mobilize. The threat of social unrest alone was a major force in prompting the CPAL to look for and find a solution. It is reasonable to expect that responsibility for social unrest in a problematic community could have created pressure on the government to review the activities and procedures of the CPAL. By accommodating through allocating benefits, by deviating from its own policy, and by not vetoing the land-use planning proposal, the CPAL assured that no interference by higher authorities would take place.

Direct involvement in both small and large community planning issues appears to lessen the ability of the CPAL to adhere strictly to a general urban land-use policy while pursuing the preservation of agricultural land. This draws the organization into the politics of planning policy. A general policy can be expressed in a general plan, which would have designated tracts of land for future urban development. Instead, its basic project-by-project approach, which was to provide some flexibility and thus overcome opposition to the declaration that all unbuilt land is agricultural, resulted in the CPAL's deep involvement in bargaining.

## Political Roles and Procedures

Procedural planning theory could explain the CPAL's behavior in as much as it develops its own mode of decision making and operational procedures. On this basis the CPAL could be expected to engage in "programmed" decision making. But the CPAL's role as a watch dog over land-use plans, its rule-making powers, and in its role as an appeal body and as a licenser, generate conflict. Programmed decisions are contingent upon receiving full information concerning courses of action and outcomes. The CPAL's legally and behaviorally recognized roles in urban development pose a number of impediments on a programmed decision procedure. Firstly, CPAL members are representatives of other organizations and are therefore likely to be inspired by the policies of their home organizations. Secondly, individual members and the organizations they represent are not free from the pressures exerted in urban and national political coalitions. Thirdly, because the CPAL generates conflict, it is also likely to be confronted by demands to make certain decisions by pressure from above or by threat of such pressure. Fourthly, in the case-by-case approach that it adopted in lieu of a general policy, the CPAL is likely to be put in a position of proving its viability and relevance to urban development planning. Lastly, the CPAL is likely to be involved in decisions that lead to confrontation with strong actors such as the Ministry of Interior or the government. These factors affect the CPAL's procedures and make it respond by either vetoing, approving or licensing — depending on the issues and actors involved. Procedures assure its viability as a power-wielding organization; deviations determine its political survival.

The CPAL is a regulative and allocative policy body. The former includes structural policies that establish rules of the game (authority structures); the latter are policies that confer or withhold direct benefits. The CPAL is involved in both, thereby creating an interactive system of different patterns of demand involving individuals, investors, land developers, municipal governments, etc. From the statutory perspective it would be expected to exhibit procedural clarity in its decisional pattern. But, as noted earlier, because of the CPAL's various modes of decision making in response to demands, a more political pattern is likely to emerge. An organization's capacity to determine its own structural policy is a clue to its influence. The regulative policy of the CPAL stems not only from the 1965 PBL, but also from the practices that it evolves. Certainly, the CPAL's regulative and allocative features account for its involvement in the politics of planning. It places it in the arena of conflict resolution, which mandates involvement in community planning, the use of resources, adaptation strategies and very often ad hoc compromises.

# Notes — Chapter 4

1. Salisbury, R.H. "The Analysis of Public Policy: A Search for Theories and Roles" in Ran, A. (ed.) *Political Science and Public Policy*. Chicago: Markham, 1968, p. 158. On the effect of structural framework, see Self, P. *Political Theories of Modern Government*. London: Allen and Unwin, 1985, esp. ch. 5.
2. Hanf, K. and Scharpf, F.W. *Interorganizational Policy Making*. London: Sage, 1978, pp. 1-115; Evan, W.M. *Organization Theory*. New York: Wiley, 1976; and Crozier, M. and Thoenig, J.C. "The Regulation of Complex Organized Systems," *Administrative Science Quarterly* 21 (1976):547-570.
3. Torgovnik, E. "Israel: The Persistent Elite" in Tachau, F. (ed.). *Political Elites and Political Development in the Middle East*. Cambridge, Mass.: Schenkman and Wiley, 1975, pp. 219-254.
4. Planning and Building Law, 1965. Jerusalem: Ministry of Interior, 1985, p. 24. Also see first amendment, p. 74.
5. *Ibid.*, p. 74, also p. 75.
6. *Ibid.*, p. 74, also p. 73.
7. *Minutes*, CPAL 19 (5 February 1968), p. 2.
8. *Ibid.*, p. 2.
9. *Ibid.*, p. 3.
10. *Ibid.* and also see criticism of these policies in *Minutes*, NPBC, 96 (4 June 1974), p. 6, and *Minutes*, CPAL (2 May 1968). Also Interview with Y. Dash, Chief Planner, Ministry of Interior.
11. *Minutes*, CPAL, 22 (22 April 1968), p. 3.
12. Interviews with E. Guzman and Y. Dash, and *Minutes*, CPAL (5 June 1969 and 19 August 1968).
13. *Minutes*, CPAL, 22 (22 April 1968), p. 4.
14. *Ibid.* and *Minutes*, CPAL (17 January 1968), p. 5.
15. *Minutes*, CPAL, 24 (6 May 1968), p. 3.
16. *Ibid.*
17. Lowi, T. *The End of Liberalism*. New York: Norton, 1969, p. 301.
18. *Minutes*, CPAL, 22 (22 April 1968), p. 3 and 24 (6 May 1968).
19. *Ibid.*, 22, p. 3.
20. *Ibid.*, p. 3.
21. *Ibid.*, p. 3.
22. *Ibid.*, p. 4.
23. *Ibid.*, p. 4.

24. Yad is a pseudonym. Interviewed officials requested not to mention their community by name. Its regional location is identified.
25. Letter of the local planning commission (Sharon-South) to the CPAL (25 April 1970).
26. *Minutes*, CPAL (5 June 1971); cf. *Minutes*, CPAL, 22 (22 April 1968).
27. Supreme Court of Israel, Local Committee vs. the CPAL. (324/71), 27, 1, p. 85, 89.
28. *Ibid.*, p. 90.
29. *Ibid.*, p. 90.
30. *Ibid.*, p. 90.
31. Supreme Court of Israel, Local Committee vs. the CPAL (445/71), 27, 2, p. 296. Also see no. (602/75).
32. Supreme Court of Israel, Litur vs. the CPAL (445/71), 31, 1, p. 103. Also no. (602/175) and *Haaretz* (11 November 1976).
33. Supreme Court of Israel, Local Committee vs. the CPAL (601/75).
34. *Minutes*, CPAL, 25 (6 May 1968).
35. *Minutes*, CPAL, 30 (19 August 1968).
36. *Ibid.*
37. *Ibid.*
38. *Ibid.*, p. 116.

# Chapter 5

# CENTRAL-LOCAL PARALLEL PLANNING

In this chapter the dominant role of the state in urban planning policy is considered by explicating the initiation, enactment and implementation of planning development policy in Jerusalem. Analysis focuses on the confrontations between urban master planning and what we call parallel planning — which involves open competition for dominance in planning policy, in a given physical area, between the state and the urban center. In this chapter (using data on Jerusalem), and in the following chapter (using data on Tel Aviv), analysis makes salient this competition and the role therein of societal goals. Parallel planning is shown to be the vehicle for the expression of state goals and the state's competition with local urban planning.

## The Setting for Conflict

Master planning generally involves low conflict and is likely to elicit a high level of agreement among professional and political elites. It has built-in flexibility and assures contestants that their views are heard, and that their values are represented or can be incorporated. In contrast, parallel planning involves competition, intense action, and conflict. It involves much uncertainty regarding goals, and its major concern is the expeditious translation of planning to implementation. Master planning indicates only a broad commitment to a specific planning policy. Because the actions of parallel planning tend to negate some of the rules of the game of planning procedures and policy, it elicits reactive political behavior. The goals of the Jerusalem master plan were in conflict with parallel planning. What was involved in Jerusalem was an urban system's effort to return to control, an effort to re-legitimize procedure and rule in order to control substantive planning policy. Under high pressure situations, and when the powers of the state are activated to achieve desired goals and particular courses of action, this conflict generating situation is most likely to reflect the dominant planning policy ideology and be supported by the political lead of the time. Parallel planning politics is somewhat idiosyncratic in its deviation from the structured planning policy game, but it has universal features: (1) the use of the power of the state vis-a-vis the local urban system when important stakes are involved; and (2) an identifiable network of actors involving political leaders, planners, public officials, interest groups, and others with access to planning policy.

The parallel planning that took place in Jerusalem underscores the limited power in planning policy initiation attributed to professional planners. The perspective revealed here is that of a local urban struggle for the institutionalization of its role in planning policy which had been challenged by the state. Planning policy in Jerusalem is related to the conflict between various local and national authorities over development. Blowers has stated that any interpretation of the pattern of development of land-use and urban development must investigate the relationship between national policy and local decision making.[1] This was certainly the case where Jerusalem is concerned, for its development involved deep state-urban political conflict. Underlying these relations was the national goal of domination of land acquired in the 1967 Six Day War. Before the war a master plan drawn up by the local planning authorities was viewed by planners as an opportunity for special urban planning. The war, however, changed the plans and brought them into conflict with national government politicians, ministries, and the government as a whole. The Jerusalem data underscore the idea that planning policy, like any other kind of public local-central policy issue, is determined by politics.

Planning policy evolvement involves a series of interactions among various groups, individuals and organizations over an issue or planning decision. It makes salient contest, pressure, conflict, alliance building, use of resources and modes of conflict management that are prevalent and ubiquitous in all stages and facets of planning. Data on Jerusalem reveals an important political question: What type of planning issues cause intense interaction and conflict, and what type of planning issues are likely to generate strong involvement in the political-planning arena (i.e., in the various stages of planning — inception, drafting, enactment and implementation). And what makes salient a variety of networks of individuals and organizations? Thus knowledge of specific motivations, issues and situations that generate involvement are expected to bring forth understanding of the politics of planning. It is generally agreed that the stakes an actor has are likely to determine his involvement in an issue.[2] But stakes alone are not sufficient to determine an outcome. An actor's accessibility to and availability of political resources, relative to others, is more likely to divulge who and how one might influence an outcome. Analysis of planning policy in Jerusalem will show that commitment to a policy is likely to increase an actor's stake and involvement in the policy, and generate the mobilization of resources and utilization of the systemically provided access. Differential commitments are likely to provide varying intensities of involvement. For example, in the development planning policy of the Tel Aviv L-plan (chapter 6) the Ministry of Housing played a minor role; in the parallel action oriented planning of Jerusalem the ministry was fully involved on behalf of the state preferences.

## The Major Actors

Before the 1967 war the city was committed to the Jerusalem master plan. The purpose of the plan was (1) to forestall national involvement in the politically important city, and (2) to act as a guide to local policy. This kind of commitment is an ideological stake for a planning organization; it means that the city has a clear idea about its future. Following the 1967 Six Day War the occupied land areas in the north, south and east of Jerusalem were annexed to the city. The local planning authorities were confronted by the Ministry of Housing, with its huge financial resources and a willingness to take an active role in the initiation and drafting of plans and their implementation in these areas. To build up the areas surrounding Jerusalem would implement a preferred normative position that reflected state policy of "Judaizing" Jerusalem (the Hebrew term is *Yehud Yerushalaim*). To take a leading role in this would lend much prestige, and a budget, to the ministry. The underlying factor, however, was the commitment of the state. The unclear formal status of the areas, the strong stake of the Ministry of Housing, and the view of the Jewish Jerusalem society were elements which would support an assessment by an actor that his involvement would in all likelihood be beneficial. Thus, from the outset the planning of Jerusalem involved powerful organizations with stakes in the outcome, resources at their disposal, and differential probabilities of success. The planning-policy conflict focuses not only on the initiation, enactment and implementation stages, but also concerns the outcomes of planning policy. The focus on parallel planning policy in the post-war period shows the real world of intense planning: activation of resources by a variety of local and national actors. The varied degrees of interaction and intensity of conflict is related to the extent of technical professional involvement, scope of political contest, actors' political commitment, and the use of resources.

Under parallel planning policy in Jerusalem a number of organizations made efforts to halt each others' initiation efforts and alternatively to advance their own. Examining these parallel planning efforts shows up the variety of political commitments and involvements in the stages of planning. The process from initiation to enactment and implementation will be related here to systemic structural[3] and normative features.[4] Jerusalem provides the setting for a distinction between action-oriented planning, where planning policy ends are vague or defined loosely in ideological terms, and end-oriented planning, where planning is used to define goals. Lastly, the special attitudes and motivations which the planning of Jerusalem generated provides the opportunity to examine the role of individuals, especially planners.

## Central-Local Competition

The uniqueness of Jerusalem, as many observers point out, is in its being a holy city, a city which "expresses spiritual values." A. Kutcher summarizes Jerusalem's link to its environment: "Jerusalem's spiritual essence is inextricably bound up with her visual, tangible qualities."[5] L. Mumford provides an even more encompassing view of the city: "Jerusalem holds a special place as a holy city...it became the active spiritual center of three world religions. Thus, it stands for certain cosmic insights and human values...that now embrace, in some degree, all who consciously participate in the human adventure....I feel that in Jerusalem, not merely the fate of Israel, but the destiny of the world in the centuries to come, may actually be at stake."[6]

Given these opinions it is not surprising that the politics of the planning of Jerusalem sometimes borders on warfare among those who deem themselves fit to shape her character.

In the twentieth century, plans for the city tried to express this spiritual essence through visual serenity. The Maclean plan of 1919 was the first major planning effort for Jerusalem in modern times; it called for the Old City to be separated from the rest of the city by a wide strip of landscaping, and for construction in nearby areas to be strictly controlled. A second plan (1923) emphasized green and open areas; it decentralized working and living areas, and did not even mention commercial places. In 1934, the Halliday plan reduced the green area surrounding the Old City, but declared it to be a nature reserve, not merely a green belt. A commercial center was planned along the Jaffa road axis, and more green areas were added. The 1945 Kendall plan halved the strip around the Old City to a width of about 1400 feet, and expanded the commercial areas. These plans, which evolved under the British Mandate, infringed on open space and permitted creeping urbanization.

Israel's planning of Jerusalem began soon after the state was established in 1948. The first plan followed the thinking of the Mandate plans; it emphasized flatness, decentralization, and a green belt around the Old City, and most important, it considered the city as a whole. The Rau plan, according to Kutcher, was open, horizontal, nucleated, introverted and hierarchic.[7] The topography of Jerusalem, poetically described in the Psalms as a city surrounded by hills, was most likely a major inspiration. By 1949, however, the city of Jerusalem was divided by barbed wire, with the Old City under Jordanian control and the western part under Israel's. Despite the difficulties of a divided city, the planning for the Israeli part of Jerusalem continued. A 1959 plan deferred to the character of Jerusalem by emphasizing relatively low buildings in order to preserve the skyline, and a modest road program. But actual construction showed that little attention was given to leaving open space around the Old City; by 1967 only a narrow strip of open land remained around a major part of the Old City on both the Israeli and Jordanian sides.

Even before 1967 the importance of Jerusalem to Israelis assured that the national government would be involved in its planning, and that national goals would attempt to find expression. Thus the master plan being prepared by the municipality was guided by a steering committee, which was comprised of representatives of various national bodies as well as of the municipal government. To expect planning under these circumstances to be based solely on local urban or professional considerations is unrealistic; it is more relevant to view planning as a political outcome.

The 1967 war changed the physical facts in the area. Now Israel was in control of all of Jerusalem and there was massive political pressure to reestablish Jerusalem as a unified city. The new goal raised new motivations in planning, activated various actors, revived slack resources, and resulted in parallel planning efforts. Kutcher views the involvement of politics in planning as unfortunate. He fails to see that on most policy issues there are contending forces that strive for dominance. Even the dimension of spirituality cannot automatically take precedence in the planning of a holy city; it has to compete with other values, such as nationalistic considerations and economic development. A major determinant of land-use policy in Jerusalem was the state's desire to quickly establish its permanent control over the unified city. It was inevitable that the physical planning would express this competition.

## The 1968 Master Plan

The 1968 master plan for Jerusalem was prepared by consultant architects, who do most of the planning in Israel. The planning unit was headed by the city engineer (the chief city planner), which is the practice in most of Israel's major cities. The planners set two goals: (1) to create physical conditions that would enable comfortable, pleasant and efficient urban activities, and (2) to design the city in a way that would be consistent with Jerusalem's status as the capital of Israel and as a holy city with a unique spiritual attachment for a large part of mankind.[8] Brutzkus, for many years Israel's foremost national planner, believed that the planners meant well, but that the two goals clashed: "They sacrificed the second goal in order to create conditions for the first."[9]

The goal of pleasant and efficient urban living apparently meant that the planners did not approach the planning of Jerusalem differently from that of any other city. But a goal of such a general nature does not allow for any meaningful discussion of alternatives. And while it is common (and perhaps necessary) for a planning policy that affects so many people and interests to be defined in vague terms, in the case of Jerusalem the planners proceeded as though specific goals were really agreed on. By contrast, the goals for the new city of Milton Keynes, in England, included specific details such as easy movement, good communications, balance and variety, and attractiveness. Levin suggests that such goals allow planners to treat the planning process as purely technical (i.e., non-political), a view most likely to be acceptable to the proponents of Procedural Planning Theory.[10]

The 1968 master plan for Jerusalem called for (1) a triangular business district to supplement the linear Jaffa road axis; (2) increased density and activity in the central business district; (3) few structural constraints on motorized traffic; (4) dense residential areas; (5) a network of roads and interchanges; and (6) development toward the southwest and southeast. With this aggressive plan for developing Jerusalem into a metropolitan area the planners hoped to combine the above proposals with the low-key qualities as outlined in previous plans. But many of the new goals were obviously incompatible with the old guidelines.

In the early 1960s the municipality's planners were working on a comprehensive plan (for the next 50 years), often referred to as the 2010 plan. But after the re-unification of the city in 1967 the need for a shorter time span was recognized, and this was set at 15 years. The following developments were forecast.

### PROJECTED DEVELOPMENT OF JERUSALEM (1967)[a]

|  | 15 years | 50 years | Actual[b] 1985 |
|---|---|---|---|
| Population | 600,000 | 890,000 | 458,000 |
| Labor force | 220,000 | 330,000 | 292,000[c] |
| Dwelling units | 318,000 | 1,100,000 | 128,000 |
| Number of cars per 1000 population | 360 | 425 | 119 |

Sources: (a) Jerusalem Master Plan, 1967, pp. 12, 18.
        (b) Central Bureau of Statistics, *Local Governments in Israel* No. 798. Ministry of Interior, Jerusalem, pp. 102, 18, 29, 65.
        (c) Central Bureau of Statistics, *Statistical Abstract of Israel*. Jerusalem, 1985, pp. 11, 36, 318, 464, 526.

The sudden surge in the city's population after the Six Day War, which was the basis for these estimates, necessitated an elaborate construction program of housing, offices, industry and major roads. The decision to turn Jerusalem and its surrounding villages and towns into a major urban center was clearly stated in the municipality's interim report of the master plan, which also noted that if Tel Aviv remained the nation's center for these activities it would continue to overshadow Jerusalem. This concern over the centrality of the city was reflected in a promise to increase housing opportunities inside the city so that no suburbanization would take place.[11]

Although discussion in parts of the interim report implied that the master plan was merely a response to natural developments, the goals of the plan included structural features that would change the character of the city: increased housing density, extension of the central business district, a network of roads, and a major highway to Tel Aviv. It was clearly unreasonable to expect that the unique features of the city and the serenity of the historical sites could be preserved when the goal of urban development was set out in such clear and uncompromising terms.

The Ministry of Housing quickly took advantage of the unclear status of the newly acquired areas to become involved not only in planning, but also in implementing its own plans. There were obvious pressures to build in Jerusalem: the unification of the city brought out a dormant feeling of nationalism, public institutions announced plans to transfer to Jerusalem, and many people decided to move there. The ministry could easily predict that its construction in Jerusalem would be accepted, even if it bypassed normal planning procedures and ignored the city's primary role in planning. In contrast to the city's attempt to formulate broad planning goals through the master plan, the ministry's planning was specific and action-oriented. The goal was defined in ideological terms — to increase the Jewish population of the unified city.

## Action-Oriented Planning and the Value of Procedure

A nationalistic ideology makes it possible to bypass normal procedures. The emphasis is on quick results which appear to fulfill popular expectations. Institutionalized procedures often fail to meet the challenges of sudden change; some organizations may have to give way so that others can meet the challenges. The planning efforts of the city of Jerusalem can be related to a process of institutionalization in which organizations and procedures struggle to acquire value and stability, but the process as a whole constrained the city.

Under normal circumstances the clash of conflicting values in planning is inevitable; under unusual conditions it is intense. In the context of a re-unified city, and a systemic preference for its Judaization, organizations chose to rely not on regular planning procedure but rather on trade-offs with other actors. In Jerusalem, the zero sum approach dominated. Construction of housing by the government without competitive planning in newly acquired areas created a commitment to this course, in this way eliminating compromise and accommodation features. Planning organizations became obsolete in the new situation in which higher authorities were involved. It is perhaps self-evident that agencies and groups that interact in unusual intensities often, both initially and throughout the conflict, promote contradictory values. The conflict in Jerusalem reflected the conflict within society: the city attempted to preserve procedure and slow master and outline planning, while the Ministry of Housing was engaged in action-oriented planning and implementation.

Schattschneider notes that a stronger conflict tends to overshadow a lesser conflict. In Jerusalem, the stronger conflict was generated by the government's efforts to expand the Jewish population of the city as rapidly as possible; the lesser conflict for the government was over planning procedures and professional planning norms.[12] The government immediately developed two areas without any real coordination with the local planning and building commission. One was Ramat Eshkol, and an area northeast of Jerusalem known as French Hill. The government was not seriously concerned with planning procedure, although its actions influenced it. Indeed, because of the haste with which these neighborhoods were built-up, the city and Ministry of Housing were long afterward debating who should pay for the infrastructure.

There was little left of planning procedure in Jerusalem. The Treasury issued an administrative order to establish ownership of the land by the Land Management Authority. The Ministry of Housing would ask the municipality for quick approval of 3,000 dwelling units; and a compromise would be reached on 2,400 units. No serious efforts were made to integrate such planning in the master or outline plans. The Ministry of Housing, which controlled vast resources, immediately began elaborate infrastructure work in French Hill, and negotiated with investors and potential buyers. The development came to the attention of the local and regional planning and building commissions only after work had already begun, even though legally and procedurally it is the responsibility of the LPBC to outline infrastructure projects, and that of the RPBC to approve and supervise the implementation of local plans. Approval by the RPBC came only after the fact.

The RPBC attempted to force a return to regular procedure by demanding that the LPBC stop the work on the infrastructure until the planning implications were considered. The local commission chose not to do so, arguing that high-level political considerations were involved. The RPBC was entitled to appropriate the LPBC's authority and act on its behalf, but chose not to do so. Neither were the plans considered in the light of an urban conception or alternative plans. After about eight months of work the Ministry of Housing finally submitted its plan for the area, but only after the project was well established. Because the structure of the RPBC is composed of many representatives of government agencies, it was relatively easy to obtain approval. In the RPBC, representatives of the Ministry of Housing and representatives of other governmental agencies could advocate in favor of the plans of the Ministry of Housing, even though the plans were not fully considered by the LPBC.

By the time the Ministry of Housing's development plans were brought before the local and regional planning and building commissions it was too late to discuss them in the broad framework of a master plan or to offer alternatives. All that the commissions could do was to deal with aspects such as the character of the housing projects and the extent of community services. Once the major land-use decision had been appropriated by the government, the function of local planning was reduced to making decisions on technique. The representatives of national ministries functioned as direct representatives of dominant norms and the government's position. They did not act as decision makers guided by planning principles.

The forced growth of Jerusalem, resulting from the national government's parallel planning and development projects, increased the city's financial and service problems. The government appointed a special committee to consider ways of helping the city carry the burden which had been thrust upon it. The special committee inadvertently portrayed the LPBC as being against a clear societal goal — the expansion of Jewish Jerusalem. But this had not been the city's intention at all; on the contrary, the post-1967 master plan set aggressive goals for growth. The city had simply tried to uphold planning goals and procedure, but this was viewed as obstructive to national policy. Data here indicate that procedural planning concepts cannot be a guide for action, neither can planning policy be viewed as the exclusive domain of any one group, organization or individual. As Wilson warned: "If urban planning is about society achieving its goals, then the main issue about planning is whether the professional planner can link society sufficiently and effectively to insure that it is society's goals which are being achieved and not his own."[13]

Since the development of Jerusalem involved national goals and enjoyed immense popularity, the "technicalities" of planning procedure were taken for granted. Historically, procedure rarely played an important role in the Israeli experience. Even during the pre-state period, the establishment of many new settlements was carried out contrary to procedure or formal legality. The justification was that the moral issue of nation building superseded the value of procedure, or even of strict legality. At that time the illegal immigration of survivors of the Nazi death camps was viewed in the same light.

## The Bases of Deviation

National political considerations, such as an increased Jewish presence in Jerusalem, is one factor that led to the negation of procedure. Other factors included the state's need for foreign investment and tourism projects. In Israel it was not uncommon for the Ministries of Tourism and Finance to enter into agreements with foreign investors who wanted to build a high-rise hotel on a site formally designated as a public area. Such plans are submitted to the local and regional commissions, where they are usually rejected. The ministries then argue that they have made commitments to the investors, and that the country is in dire need of the foreign currency that these investors would bring into the country. The ministries are often supported by local interests; the city of Jerusalem itself agreed to some tourism projects which clearly deviated from plans.[14]

Another reason for the lack of deference to planning procedures concerns technical and administrative competence. The RPBC often faces severe professional competition. For example, when major projects are submitted by the Ministry of Transportation or the Division of Public Works, the RPBC faces organizations that have highly competent professional staffs. This results in a power imbalance. For example, when the major highway from Tel Aviv to Jerusalem was constructed, the regional commission was involved only marginally.

But planning organizations are not always helpless. When the Hebrew University developed its Mt. Scopus campus in 1968 the work was carried out, at the insistence of the local and regional planning and building commissions, in accordance with the master plan. Appeals to the Prime Minister to pressure the planning commissions were to no avail; the view and the green belt were preserved, open spaces, building heights and other details were coordinated through the LPBC.[15]

Action-oriented planning appears to involve the negation of procedures. Even when an organization follows prescribed procedures at some stage of their implementation, it remains a part of the concept of parallel planning. The actual building permits for certain spots in French Hill were issued after the fact. This is classified as action-oriented planning because of its loose relation to the city's plans, because of the initial deviations, and especially because the parallel planning process was apparent. Thus, the city's role in the conflict involved a struggle for a return to procedure and the domination of substance.

## Local Strategies

The intensity of the conflict over the planning of Jerusalem is related to the Israeli political culture. Israel is known for its proclivity to act pragmatically now and face consequences later; to establish facts in disputed areas (sometimes without regard to procedure), and to defend them with their lives afterwards. But little has been said about the motivation for this pattern of behavior. The establishment of scores of settlements along the borders of Israel during the past 40 years is an indication of the dynamism of Israelis. However, it also reflects an underlying fear of dispossession. Israelis feel compelled to prove, perhaps more to themselves than their adversaries, the fact of their existence and their entrenchment in the land of Israel. And this element was probably the dominant fact behind the emphasis on parallel action, and the rapid growth and development in the action-oriented planning of Jerusalem.

In the narrow legal sense, the newly acquired territories surrounding Jerusalem did not fall under the jurisdiction of the local or regional planning and building commissions; nevertheless, it was apparent that the territories would eventually be incorporated within the municipal boundaries, and thus their planning should have been controlled by the local bodies. But the government ministries wanted to apply special norms to the planning of Jerusalem as an excuse for using non-standard planning policy and procedures. The special situation was declared to be the uniqueness and holiness of the city; the undeclared norm was the political entrenchment of Israel in Jerusalem. There was general agreement that Jerusalem was different; however, as the undeclared political goal became more apparent, the local authorities tried to regain their predominant authority over the planning of Jerusalem, and this was the essence of the conflict.

## Professionals as a Resource

Mayor Kollek of Jerusalem set up an advisory committee, known as the Jerusalem Committee, of internationally prominent planners and architects, in order to comment on the city's plans. The mayor wanted the plan to become the accepted definition of goals, and he assessed that the Ministry of Housing would find it difficult to ignore the opinion of such a blue-ribbon panel. The Jerusalem Committee was thus expected to reinforce the municipality's planning authority, even though the international committee was itself also a deviation from regular planning procedure.

The city's plans outlined development to the south and east, that is in the direction of the territories acquired in the Six Day War. Thus, it reflected the dominance of national political considerations. The Jerusalem Committee, which included such figures as Mumford, Kahn, Mayerowitz, Halperin, Safdi, Swee and Johnson, faced the difficult task of making professional comments on plans which involved controversial political goals. The committee criticized the push for urban development instead of limiting or preventing it, the emphasis on "trend planning" instead of on principles, the close proximity of the new and the old, and the massive arterial transportation.[16]

Mumford argued that urban growth could be controlled. However, the decision to expand had been made by the government, not by the city; in making this decision the government chose to ignore the adverse effects of rapid growth. Mumford also criticized the transportation system because it featured open transfer and accessibility rather than inner character.[17] Halperin spoke out against the emphasis on motorized transportation and the dangers of environmental pollution; he pointed to the folly of attempting to compete with Tel Aviv. Swee argued against the plastic imitation of old-style architecture, and even compared it to Mussolini's patriotic construction.[18] Safdi was critical of the lack of non-motorized alternatives for transportation. Mayerowitz warned against the urban ills implicit in the plan; Kahn criticized the disregard for the spiritual aspects of Jerusalem. Several Israeli planners criticized the neglect of the city center, the grandiose features which did not take cost into account, and the secretive atmosphere which cloaked the planning.[19]

It was unusual to see such extensive criticism of public policy in Israel, especially of urban issues. The heated debate that ensued was a result of the special feelings that Jerusalem invokes, and of the expectation that Jerusalem would be treated differently from other cities. It was triggered by the Jerusalem Committee which, in regard to the mayor's purpose in setting up the committee, was both functional and dysfunctional. The criticism did not help eliminate parallel planning, but it did help generate more sensitivity among the planners. Eylon, a columnist and author, summarized the criticism: (1) the rapid settling of Arab territories was not what would convince international institutions to accept them as Jewish; (2) "fear dominated the planning," which was likely to result in physical monsters that continued old notions of planning; and (3) patriotism and nationalism, not urbanism, dominated the planning of Jerusalem.[20] Israel's decision-making structure is generally quite immune to public criticism, unless it comes from within the political structure. The mayor hoped the criticism of the Jerusalem Committee, the Israeli urban experts and the press would make some of the decision-making organizations ally with the city. Kollek used the criticisms not so much to correct planning, but rather as a lever in his relations with these organizations. Speaking before the international committee the mayor described his strategy of fighting parallel planning by inviting the members to scrutinize plans. "The people who came here...really tried not so much to *solve* the problems of Jerusalem, but to *save* in Jerusalem what they...had lost in many other cities, which were irretrievably spoiled." Speaking before the international committee he found himself inadvertently defending the state's position. The criticism of the Committee, so he argued, was a bit exaggerated. Referring to the recommended reduction in the roads planned around the Old City, he said: "Complicated and concrete situations...cannot be solved only by a nostalgic view of the city held by many of the planners. We are approaching a growth rate of 4 percent, so preserving good planning is a very complicated thing."[21] The mayor wanted to focus on the city's master plan and the local goals set therein as a focal point and as a base for reasserting the city's planning role. If the city received support for the goals outlined in the master plan it would have the leeway to translate them into a binding outline plan. This, of course, would be a blend of nostalgia and urban development.

The national government's motivation for taking a strong role in the planning of Jerusalem was reflected in the many ad hoc organizations that were established and their flagrant deviation from procedure. Not all of the organizations involved are mentioned here, but a partial listing is sufficient to underscore the point that planning policy emerged as a result of parallel planning, and its accompanying conflict and resolution.

An ad hoc coordinating ministerial committee, which included the mayor of Jerusalem, was established right after the 1967 war to give quick approval to construction in the newly-acquired territories, especially in the Old City.[22]

There was an interministerial committee, comprising the directors-general of the various ministries, as well as an administrative committee, which corresponded to the coordinating ministerial committee. The administrative committee was established under the emergency law and given the power to bypass regular planning institutions.[23]

Not all of these organizations survived the long contest, but each played a role at different stages. As a result of the involvement of so many decision organizations there were several sets of plans — for example, the master plan, the transportation plan, the Old City plan, and the Ministry of Housing's plan. The planning and implementation took place in different forums, which made it difficult for the local and regional planning and building commissions to relate to one cohesive plan or to deal with one group of planners. The major planning policy struggle concerning the Old City was seized, for example, by the city of Jerusalem in order to re-establish the municipality as the prime mover of the planning and development of Jerusalem. The struggle also points to the process of parallel planning, namely when a government decision gave the Ministry of Interior the authority to become involved in the planning of the Old City. The plan was prepared by special staff who were not directly under the jurisdiction of the city, but were appointed by the Ministry of Interior. The plan called for an avenue some 150 feet wide to connect the Old City, the central business district, and the government office enclave. Even within the ministry there was little consensus. The chief planner of the Ministry of Interior opposed the road, which he felt would destroy the features of the Old City by integrating the picturesque city into a major urban development program.[24] The mayor of Jerusalem pressured the Minister of Interior, who finally agreed in principle to do away with the special planning body, on the condition that it not be dissolved until a year after approval of the plan. In this way the ministry held it as a threat of potential interference over the city. The municipality, using its LPBC and the RPBC, received special powers over the planning of the Old City and in this way retained a role in the planning.[25]

## Domination in the Planning of Jerusalem

Influence is the ability to prevent other people's policies from being enacted, and to initiate and implement policies in spite of opposition.[26] When the Ministry of Housing initiated its plans and began actual implementation of construction, it relied on the approval of the ad hoc administrative and coordinating committees to bypass the city of Jerusalem. But as the city re-established its role in planning it had to confront a stronger city which had become more organized and clearer about its planning goals; the planning outcomes were then determined by whether the ministry could dominate the conflict and interaction with the city and other organizations.

To retain some leverage the government held on to the special legal status of the newly acquired territories, but at the same time had to give in to the city's demands for control of planning. A special committee for construction in the newly-acquired areas was set up in 1970, with the mayor of Jerusalem as chairman and the city planner as a member; this was the first step in the return of planning authority to the city. The other members were representatives from the Ministry of Justice, the Land Management Authority, and the Ministry of Interior. Nevertheless, use was still made of the old British Mandate Emergency Laws in order to cut red tape. This was preferable to simply disregarding the wishes of the city council, established procedure, and legal norms. It indicated that the deviations were acceptable, but under some legal framework. Under the emergency laws, policy outputs would have the validity of plans approved by the LPBC and RPBC.[27] The irony was that the Jewish presence in Jerusalem would be increased by using a law designed by the British to suppress Jewish settlement during the British Mandate period.

The Ministry of Interior, via its representative on the special committee, opposed the use and the attempt to institutionalize deviation from procedure and legality through emergency laws; it was afraid that this would become the accepted norm and reduce its own traditional role in planning in the RPBC. An interministerial conflict ensued against the background of varied on-going planning and implementation. The attorney-general of Israel intervened to face a demand by the Ministry of Housing for more authority for the special administrative committee to enable it to bypass the LPBC and the RPBC. The Ministry of Interior reacted by threatening not to approve such a deviation. The outcome was that the committee would be only a coordinating committee, and would not have the power to approve building plans. This set the stage for a return to legality and procedure, and enabled the city to assume a key role in the planning of the city.

Nevertheless, because the coordinating committee was given the authority to approve the infrastructure for the new area, the Ministry of Housing emerged from the conflict quite strong. That meant that it was allowed to begin various projects, and in Israel's administrative culture this meant the right to complete. The decision also sanctioned major deviations from procedure and the role of political competition in planning. Other organizations were unable to halt the initiatives of the Ministry of Housing, although it eventually would have to face the local and regional planning bodies. The ministry's main resource was in raising the specter of the international political threat to the Jewish presence in Jerusalem, and it was difficult to disregard this argument. The American government reprimanded Israel for its construction in east Jerusalem, and very critical articles appeared in the *New York Times*. The Ministry of Housing used this international criticism as a major resource in its efforts for delaying urban planning, which thereby left it free to decide and implement its own ad hoc plans. Thus, foreign criticism was an important resource by one actor in the conflict with the city and it hindered the city's planning role and its attempts to control implementation of planning and development.

The standardized and ordinary looking housing that now covers a great part of the new areas of Jerusalem may be attributed partly to the American Rogers' Peace Plan, which threatened the political status of Jerusalem. In response to the American peace initiative, Prime Minister Meir ordered the fastest possible construction and settlement in east Jerusalem.[28] Legitimate urban planning criticism was easily dismissed as being a dovish political position in disguise. The haste (and panic) with which government officials encouraged the Ministry of Housing's construction without comprehensive planning was a transfer of past practice to the present; when Israelis purchased land, built and settled it, the area remained Israeli. But in the case of Jerusalem this was not really relevant. The American plan for Jerusalem did not speak of territorial divisions between Arabs and Jews, but economic, religious and administrative (i.e., functional) divisions.

The small shift back toward local control of substantive planning, legality and procedure that did occur was due purely to the organizational interests of the city and the Ministry of Interior, both of which realized that the special committee could strip them of powers in the planning of Jerusalem.

## Overcoming the City's Opposition

The Ministry of Housing became the most dominant actor in the planning and implementation of policy in Jerusalem because it had the powerful resource of government support for its construction plans. Had it not been for the special coordinating committee, the ministry's construction would have proceeded without any restraint from the LPBC and RPBC. Public, professional and international criticism could not stop the Ministry of Housing from implementing the entrenchment of Israel in the Jerusalem area.

Rapid construction took place in the hills surrounding Jerusalem. The Ministry of Housing began to build the infrastructure in Nebi Samuel. After this huge investment it was only a matter of time before its plans for the construction of dense public housing in the area would proceed. The city opposed the plans on several grounds: (1) they were not coordinated with the city and were inconsistent with its goals; (2) the distance of Nebi Samuel from the rest of the city would involve immense expenditures for the provision of municipal services; (3) leap-frog development did not follow the natural development tendencies of the city; (4) high-density construction on the hilltops would destroy the visual beauty and serenity of Jerusalem's environment.

The issue also involved public debate. Criticism in the press was relentless; very few favored rapid construction because of international political considerations. The issue also reached the Knesset because the local and regional planning and building commissions attempted to block any construction beyond that of the infrastructure. The Knesset debate took place only a week before plans were submitted to the RPBC for approval. The Ministry of Housing mobilized the head of the country's largest construction company (owned by the Histadrut), whose populist rhetoric supported the plan. He argued that the shortage of housing in Jerusalem increased its cost to the people, and that dense construction in Nebi Samuel would alleviate this problem. This was a pure political support position by an economic interest, because cheaper housing could be obtained through non-controversial projects. In addition, the company had an obvious and direct interest in construction projects (which were handed out by the Ministry of Housing). In general, the Knesset followed the Prime Minister's lead and supported the position of the ministry.[29]

The Ministry of Housing, through Minister Sherf, answered the city's criticism of the lack of comprehensive coordinated planning expected under the hierarchical structure of the 1965 PBL by pointing to the high quality technical planning work by architects/planners who had been working for over a year on plans for Nebi Samuel and other areas. This, of course, did not negate the fact that such planning was parallel planning — isolated from the city planning of Jerusalem. The ministry threatened that if the LPBC did not approve the plans, the city might remain divided ethnically and he would bring the issue before the government, which could go ahead with planning and construction under the emergency laws. Minister Sherf claimed that even the government wanted the hills around Jerusalem to be covered with housing projects, and not to remain green suburbs and semi-villages.[30]

The mayor of Jerusalem was involved in this debate, but he opposed the ministry's plans with a faint voice. He realized that it would be difficult to refute the nationalistic argument. *Haaretz* declared: "He (the mayor), who should have stood at the head of the movement to defend Jerusalem from those who want to turn her into an ugly city, is silent. There is an impression that he is bent on using the public excitement over the hasty construction of Jerusalem against urban and planning principles in order to succeed in getting a few million pounds out of the Treasury for Jerusalem."[31] This, of course, was an exaggerated (if not unfair) view of the mayor's position, which was to return the planning of Jerusalem to Jerusalem.

## Planners and Their Organizations

The planners in the Ministry of Housing were expected to support their minister's position, even though they were not unanimously in favor of the ministry's policy. In chapter three we noted that planners in Israel are rarely free to take a public stand that contradicts the position of their organization. When major values are at stake, as is often the situation in planning, and was definitely the case in Jerusalem — they are allowed little leeway in their work.

Before final approval of the Nebi Samuel project by the RPBC, planners in the Ministry of Housing took a most unexpected step in Israel's political-bureaucratic culture; five of the planners went public with their opposition to the plan. They argued that nothing should be constructed before the project was assessed in relation to the city's goals as expressed in the master plan. They said that they had been working on the program against their professional conscience, under pressure from the Ministry of Housing's chief planner for Jerusalem who, they claimed, was imbued with an excitement for wild construction.[32] Their action in asserting themselves was bold and unusual, and the press applauded them. Since the Ministry of Housing is the major source of work for planners, this was a serious step for any planner to take. It signified open involvement in the politics of planning. The rebellious planners exposed plans that otherwise would have remained secret until construction was underway. Such secrecy is not unique to planning in Israel; many policy areas are developed under extreme secrecy. Were it not for a free and alert press and the proclivity of politicians to leak information in order to overcome their anonymity or gain public support for policy positions, many aspects of policy would remain unknown outside the government.[33]

It could be argued that the ministry's chief planner, in accepting and following political dictates, fulfilled his proper function as a staff man. But from a different perspective it may be argued that the dissident planners proposed that planners cannot remain just obedient administrators with technical professional skills. They entered the public arena of policy conflict, and refused to apply their expertise obediently to given goals. Rather, they wanted to shape the goals as well; from the theoretical perspective of advocacy planning, this is an acknowledged role of planners. From the procedural planning theory perspective the explanation of planners' public advocacy is less easily explicable. Another planner, in charge of the UN Palace area around Jerusalem, resigned because the planning directions given to him were against his professional conscience.[34] The planners most certainly did not accept the administrative-managerial hierarchy. Although professionals (such as scientists) require less hierarchical settings than one finds in governmental structure, public planning in Israel belongs to organizational commissions and hierarchies.

The Ministry of Housing took on the challenge of the planners and began a campaign to discredit them. Spokesmen noted that the planners had been silent for a long time, and claimed that their motivations were personal and not professional.[35] The outcome was simple and swift. A short time before the RPBC approved the Nebi Samuel plan, all five rebellious planners were dismissed for disloyalty.[36] The major cause of the minister's anger was the public position taken by the planners in fighting for their views. If the struggle had been conducted within the organizational limits of the ministry, the planners might have kept their jobs, but the effect of their protest would most likely have been nil in light of the central dominance of local planning. As it turned out, their public protest had no effect either. The Minister of Housing used physical development to gain prestige for his ministry as the creator of a full Israeli presence in Jerusalem. His frame of reference was not planning, but his position in the government. And he used his ministry to carry out the strategies of the government. If effective planning is viewed as implementing the directives of authoritative institutions, then the Ministry of Housing was an effective planner. The problem was that the other government ministries that he dealt with were not really concerned with planning per se, but had access to urban planning in Jerusalem as a part of parallel planning. Such agencies are referred to as organizations involved in planning, as distinguished from regular planning organizations such as the local and regional commissions.

The Ministry of Housing's strategy of settling Jerusalem with more Jews was based on parallel planning and the mobilization of support from higher governmental authorities. This strategy enabled the ministry to dominate the initiation and implementation stage of planning. What remains to be explicated is the approval (or enactment) stage, where the city and the regular planning organizations reestablished their roles. At this point the dominance of the state's position and the Ministry of Housing, although not eliminated, was reduced. This stage is discussed in the following sections.

## Regaining Local Authority Over Planning

In the Tel Aviv L-Plan development the city dominated the planning process from beginning to end (chapter six). But in Jerusalem the situation was more complex. The city had to cope with attempting to regain authority over the initiation and enactment of various planning organizations, planning under emergency laws, the state's commitment to parallel planning, and special legislation. It succeeded in preventing the Ministry of Housing from bypassing the LPBC. Altogether, the ministry arrived with a record of success in generating government support during the initiation stage. Nevertheless, the local and regional commissions provided an opportunity to modify the initial plans in order to bring them more in line with city and regional planning norms.

As noted in chapter three, the LPBC and RPBC are not homogeneous bodies; their members represent the various political parties and ministries. For example, the LPBC reflects the structure of the municipal government coalition. Consequently, members may take different positions on a planning issue, especially when the issue is as controversial as the Ministry of Housing's plan for the areas surrounding Jerusalem. Similarly, varied conflicts emerge in the RPBC's review of plans. This was especially significant since the Ministry of Housing is a part of the network of decision makers and has a formal role on this commission. We observed similar processes involving decisions over the Ministry of Housing's plans for Nebi Samuel, the Old City, and the UN Palace areas.

The major planning controversy involved the LPBC's demand that the Ministry of Housing's plan for Nebi Samuel be related to the city's evolved binding outline plan.[37] On numerous occasions, the LPBC's strong stand in trying to assert local authority over land area and plans led to counter action by the ministry. The government mooted the possibility of setting up a new and separate municipal entity in Nebi Samuel. In response the mayor backed off and suggested that the ministry's plans simply be modified to correspond to the city's conceptions. Another issue was the height of the proposed buildings. The local commission wanted to reduce the height so that the buildings would not be visually offensive from the road leading into Jerusalem.[38]

The city's assertiveness was tempered by its awareness of the power behind the Ministry of Housing. In discussing matters before the LPBC the deputy mayor noted that placing too many obstructions in the path of the ministry might reactivate the government's coordinating committee — a body which the city had succeeded in making dormant. He also noted that attempts by the city to compel the ministry to propose comprehensive plans for the UN Palace area had not been heeded because of "special reasons" (this alluded to the national goal of increasing Jewish population).[39] Thus the LPBC itself watered down its original success in reinstituting legality and procedure; in some instances it approved construction before detailed plans were submitted. But given the ministry's threat to ignore detailed plans altogether, the LPBC's discretion was perhaps the better part of valor.

The Ministry of Housing's plan projected a population of 30,000 to 40,000 in the Nebi Samuel area; the city's master plan foresaw 10,000 residents.[40] The ministry's chief planner suggested that the question of density be worked out between the mayor of Jerusalem and the ministry,[41] and that in the meantime the ministry's plan for the first stage be approved because it concerned only 10 percent of the area. In trying to persuade the LPBC to deal with projects instead of with an overall plan, the ministry's chief planner argued that final targets were not of immediate concern. But the deputy mayor saw through the ploy and decided to wait for the decision on density, in order to achieve additional design modification requirements such as lower level buildings and more green areas. As the process went on it became increasingly difficult for the ministry to threaten the city with removal of this issue from its jurisdiction. The LPBC became more demanding, insisting on detailed plans and models for the entire area, and compatibility with the city's master plan, especially in regard to density.

The members of the local planning commission did not always agree on what to do. There was a consensus to delay the decision on Nebi Samuel, but they were divided as to what to do with the UN Palace area. The split was between those who were concerned with the national goal of Judaizing the area and those who were more concerned with planning and local dominance, preserving a green belt, and seeing detailed plans before granting their approval of projects. This group was aided by the protracted conflict it maintained. The local conflict adversely affected Israel's desire to have its role in the expanded Jerusalem recognized internationally.

The conflict over Nebi Samuel was resolved after the mayor and the Minister of Housing agreed on the matter of density.[42] The mayor succeeded in reducing the density to 600 dwelling units in four-story buildings. The LPBC, recognizing the political urgency of the situation, agreed to have the first stage of the Nebi Samuel development prepared as a detailed, legally binding plan, but insisted that approval of any subsequent work was conditional on the Ministry of Housing's submission of an overall plan for the entire Nebi Samuel area.[43] LPBC members were satisfied with the planning policy role that they had regained. Once this had been achieved they became enthusiastic about development (the national goal), often ignoring the planners warnings about the high cost and burdens to the city of the new service delivery system that would be needed. Their view was clearly stated: "Construction on mountains (i.e., disregard for the beauty of Jerusalem's skyline) is preferable to an underdeveloped city....Cities [in Israel] were built against the opinions of experts. Had we listened to experts, the role of development in the country would have been insignificant."[44] These nationalistic and pragmatic sentiments became a policy demand for bargaining, which is often apparent in central-local relations: "The local planning and building commission of Jerusalem sees in the construction of the areas surrounding Jerusalem a prime national role which will strengthen Jerusalem. Therefore, it is the obligation of the government to assume the financial cost of the infrastructure, of public community institutions, and of other economic implications of this construction."[45] As the threat to local authority was progressively removed, local-central bargaining over resources could take place.

The LPBC passed on to the RPBC its approval of the first stage of the Nebi Samuel project, along with its demand for government aid. The agreement between the Mayor of Jerusalem and the Minister of Housing led to a united front between them over the initial plans of Nebi Samuel in the RPBC. The RPBC attempted to influence the direction of the Nebi Samuel project and the Ministry of Interior's planner used this decision arena in an effort to ban construction near the hilltops in order to preserve the skyline. Representatives of the Ministry of Transportation raised a faint voice against the program on the grounds that immediate construction would require huge sums of money for transportation and infrastructure. Representatives of the Ministry of Labor and the Ministry of Defense supported the Ministry of Housing.

The conflict with the city was resolved in the RPBC, and a central-local partnership model seemed to evolve.[46] Thus, in the RPBC the Ministry of Housing's chief planner on the Nebi Samuel project could, along with the city engineer (chief city planner), speak on behalf of the city of Jerusalem. He also spoke as the political representative of the ministry and the government as a whole. The strategy of persuasion was primarily based on planning considerations, but he also took advantage of the Israeli population's resentment of American criticism of Jewish settlement in Jerusalem: "If the people of Israel build, the buildings should be seen. We do not build shelters or ditches and holes. We are building the Hebrew Jerusalem; why shouldn't it stand out on the skyline?"[47] To the representative of the Ministry of Transportation, he retorted: "The cost of infrastructure and transportation is being considered by a special committee. The need now is to build. Your arguments sound good for the press, but they should not be taken seriously."[48] The government supported the growth of Jerusalem and the city had approved the plans. However, the regional commission's approval was by a very narrow majority.

Mayor Kollek commented: "The right to build in (greater) Jerusalem was never questioned by us (the city) or the prestigious international Jerusalem Committee; this is not what divided the city and the Ministry of Housing."[49] Rather, the conflict was over the authority of the city to supervise its own planning, even when international pressure made other bodies become politically involved in the planning. The city's authority was defined as its right to state its goals and to require that plans for specific projects follow the guidelines of the city's plans. Urban aesthetic considerations, which the city emphasized vis-a-vis the Ministry of Housing's nationalistic considerations, were the major resources used to gain city authority over planning.[50]

## Parallel Planning Reconsidered

The role of central government organizations outlined here, including the role of the Ministry of Housing, indicate that politics and the exercise of power and influence is a determinant of planning policy. Parallel planning challenges the value of procedure and introduces a high level of conflict, which dominates the politics of planning. Defense of procedure diverts attention from substance, although the conflict over procedure is in the final analysis a struggle for domination of substance. Parallel planning tends to belittle the role that planners have in the politics of planning. When major contestants are involved, planners are expected to give support to their home organizations. They are free to take a political role, but only within the anonymous confines of their organization. Their politics, which is not public, tends to be guided by rules that provide for less effectiveness in the achievement of goals. The very organizations involved in parallel planning are political and thus advocacy of professional positions by planners is likely to become counter-productive to the major political effort of the contesting planning organizations.

Parallel planning in Jerusalem indicated that the state can take a strong role in local planning policy and its implementation. But, it should be noted that under the 1965 PBL (and thus in ongoing planning), the government agencies are key actors in urban planning organizations. It is given the final word in local planning via the RPBC. This point was made in chapter three, but along with the data in this chapter it should be concluded that parallel planning is not idiosyncratic in a city such as Jerusalem. It is a part of Israeli planning policy. The political structure enables intervention. The government's degree of involvement is determined by how highly it values the stake in a planning policy issue.

# Notes — Chapter 5

1. Blowers, A. *The Limits of Power: The Politics of Local Planning Policy*. Oxford: Pergamon, 1980, p. 111.
2. Dahl, R.A. *Who Governs? Democracy and Power in an American City*. New Haven: Yale, 1961.
3. See chapter 3.
4. See chapter 2.
5. Kutcher, A. *The New Jerusalem, Planning and Politics*. London: Thames & Hudson, 1973.
6. *Ibid.*, p. 9.
7. Kutcher (1980).
8. *Master Plan of Jerusalem* (1972). Jerusalem: Ministry of Interior, p. 8.
9. Interview with E. Brutskus, past chief planner, Ministry of Interior.
10. Levin, H. *Government and the Planning Process*. London: Allen and Unwin, 1976.
11. Master Plans. Jerusalem Report. Office Master Plan, Jerusalem, p. 3.
12. Schattschneider, E.E. *The Semi-Sovereign People. A Realist's View of Democracy in America*. New York: Holt, Reinhart & Winston, 1960.
13. Wilson.
14. On the phenomenon of deviation from plans, see here chapter 3 and Alexander, E.R., Alterman, R. and Law-Yone, "Evaluating Policy Implementations: The National Statutory Planning Systems in Israel" in Diamond, J. and McLoughlin, J.B. (eds.) *Progress in Planning* 20 (1983):140.
15. *Minutes*, LPBC — Jerusalem, 43 ( January 1972), p. 43.
16. Kutcher (1973), p. 89.
17. *Haaretz* (25 December 1970).
18. *Ibid.*
19. *Maariv* (26 February 1971); *Haaretz* (29 March 1971).
20. *Haaretz* (27 November 1970).
21. City of Jerusalem, Proceeding of the International Committee Congress, Jerusalem, p. 33.
22. *Haaretz* (26, 28 April 1971).
23. *Maariv* (13 October 1970).
24. Interview with Y. Dash, Chief Planner, Ministry of Interior.
25. *Minutes*, LPBC (9 January 1976), p. 41.
26. Dahl (1961), p. 66; Blowns (1980).
27. *Haaretz* (17 September 1970).
28. *Haaretz* (26 January 1971).
29. *Haaretz* (18 February 1971).

30. *Haaretz* (7 January 1971).
31. *Ibid.*
32. *Haaretz* (9 February 1971).
33. Cf. Galnur, I., (ed.), 1977.
34. *Haaretz* (10 February 1971).
35. *Maariv* (16 February 1971).
36. *Haaretz* (17 February 1971).
37. *Minutes*, LPBC — Jerusalem, 13 (7 February 1971), pp. 89, 13.
38. *Ibid.*, p. 11.
39. *Ibid.*, p. 52.
40. *Haaretz* (18 February 1971).
41. *Maariv* and *Haaretz* (18 February 1971).
42. *Maariv* and *Haaretz* (15 February 1971).
43. *Minutes*, LPBC — Jerusalem, 73 (17 February 1971), p. 8.
44. *Ibid.*, p. 7.
45. *Minutes*, LPBC — Jerusalem, 14 (2 February 1971), p. 2.
46. *Minutes*, RPBC — Jerusalem, 19 (26 February 1971), p. 2.
47. *Haaretz* (28 February 1971).
48. *Ibid.*
49. *Minutes*, LPBC — Jerusalem, 14 (2 February 1971), p. 12.
50. *Minutes*, LPBC — Jerusalem (1 January 1971), p. 3.

# Chapter 6

# THE POLITICS OF URBAN GROWTH

This chapter focuses on development planning policy and implementation of the L-Plan area in the City of Tel Aviv. The plan covers a tract of land of approximately 1,500 acres located in the northern outskirts of the city, across the Yarkon River. The bitter political conflict that this plan generated spanned a period of 25 years — from 1945 to 1970 — when a specific plan was approved and its implementation was begun. The discussion centers on how systemic, normative features are the basis of conflict over the planning and implementation of urban growth policy. The issue makes salient the politics of local-central relations and that of the planning organizations and other organizations involved in planning. The focus of our deliberations is on power relations and the wielding of influence in the process of the making of planning policy. In particular it will be shown how the actors, their motivations and interactions, account for their involvement in planning policy conflict.

Unlike the politics of urban planning in Jerusalem, where the city fought off state intervention and insisted on having a dominant role, the City of Tel Aviv's role in planning urban growth was not questioned by competing state organizations. The major conflict involved the very issue of urban growth itself. The development plans of Tel Aviv brought forth a conflict over the essence of the urban society Israel had become. The conflict illuminated relations between national development and urbanization, in the context of a major, planned effort to assert urban primacy in a system which historically had promoted the ideology of ruralism and defined national needs and growth in non-urban terms, even though all the while it was assiduously urbanizing.

The city had to overcome (1) the designation of the L-Plan area as agricultural, (2) the national preference for population dispersal, and (3) its corollary, national security considerations. In this instance the confrontation between local-central authorities underscored the role of societal values in planning urban growth, as well as the role of political influence and its use by a variety of actors, including private groups of landowners and construction

165

interests. The conflict also highlights the interdependence of local and central authorities in the management of urban development. The involvement of a wide scope of systemic organizations and dimensions reflects the Israeli political setting. However, the analysis of the politics involved has implications for other systems with similar, unitary features.

## Landowners, Ministerial Positions and Interests

To understand the politics of planning, one must identify which actors become involved in a planning issue and why. Landowners were the major economic group that consistently pressed for the development of the L-Plan area. They demanded that the area be redesignated from an agricultural area to an urban one, and that the development plan be approved by the local and regional planning and building organizations. Without such action they could not develop or build on their property. As members of the Landowners Association (AL), a well-financed and organized group, they allied themselves with successive mayors of Tel Aviv, each one of whom saw the area's development as a major goal of his administration.

The national government was involved because the area was not planned, and part of it (about 200 acres) was national public land. The absence of an approved outline or detailed plan prevented the development of the area. The Landowners appealed to the Supreme Court in an attempt to compel the various governmental agencies to move ahead with plans which would enable them to develop their property, but this appeal was rejected. In 1946, with the support of the mayor, an outline plan for the area was approved by the LPBC. In 1947, the principles of the plan — spacious, low-density housing and various tourism projects — were supported by the RPBC. The landowners, however, wanted high-density projects and housing. In 1953, the AL again appealed to the Supreme Court, this time requesting that it order the LPBC to increase the planned density in the area. The Supreme Court rejected the appeal since questions of density are the prerogative of the local planning organizations.

The second mayor of Tel Aviv, I. Rokach, was especially active in supporting the development of the area. The General Zionists (today's Liberal party), opposed to the rural ideology of the nationally dominant Labor party, envisioned Tel Aviv as the center of economic and trade activities in Israel — as indeed it eventually became. The third mayor of Tel Aviv, M. Namir of the Labor party, also supported the development of the L-Plan area. He saw it as a basis for strengthening the city's tax base and his dominant political group (Mapai) within the Labor political power base.

Major opposition to the L-Plan stemmed from the Ministry of Agriculture, the Ministry of Interior, and an Inter-Ministerial Committee on Population Dispersal. The Ministry of Agriculture was set on obtaining the L-Plan area for its own clients. The ministry not only opposed urban sprawl and warned against disregarding agricultural needs, but also feared that the growth of Tel Aviv might lead to further growth in other cities, conceivably diverting scarce national resources to urban functions such as transportation, rather than to the rural sector. At the height of the conflict over the L-Plan area, Dayan was Minister of Agriculture and head of a secessionist group, the Rafi faction, within the Labor party. Even prior to the formation of the Rafi faction, Dayan belonged to a group that evolved out of the opposition to the Mapai (Labor) party leadership of which Namir, the then-mayor of Tel Aviv, was a part. His opposition to the plan was primarily based on his role as Minister of Agriculture. But not to be ignored was the fact that he saw a chance to embarrass Mayor Namir, an important member of Mapai's political machine. Namir and his Tel Aviv political supporters were urban representatives, and much of their power within Mapai came from their control of the city's political machine and its link to urban voters.

The Ministry of Interior, which oversaw all planning, including urban development, argued against the excessive urban concentration implied in the plan. When the ministry was headed by Bar-Yehuda, arguments against the development of the L-Plan focused on the need to preserve the area for agricultural use, as well as the need for a "green belt." Minister Bar-Yehuda was a member of the leftist Mapam (an ally of the Labor party) whose main political base had traditionally been the kibbutzim (collective agricultural settlements). When the Ministry of Interior was later headed by Shapira, leader of the National Religious party, less emphasis was placed on sectorial (i.e., agricultural) considerations and more on the concept of a "green belt," and on the desire to implement the national population dispersal policy which the Ministry of Interior had devised.

Conflict with the Ministry of Interior was expected in any case. A large city such as Tel Aviv, and a ministry that oversees planning for the entire country, are likely to confront one another over planning issues. For example, the city's desire to increase its tax base conflicted with the ministry's goal of emphasizing "green belts" and population dispersal. In addition, when the government decided to reinforce the political position of Jerusalem as the capital of Israel, competition between the Tel Aviv municipality and the central government intensified, as Tel Aviv's reputation as a commercial center was threatened by Jerusalem's growth.

The forces of opposition to the L-Plan mobilized the Inter-Ministerial Committee on Population Dispersal, chaired by the strong and popular Prime Minister Ben-Gurion. Because part of the land belonged to the government, this committee had to give its approval to any land-use plan in the L-Plan area. Ben-Gurion, who consistently promoted the development of the remote areas of the country, the Negev desert, etc., opposed the development of the L-Plan. Only later, after Ben-Gurion retired and Eshkol, a pragmatic and development-oriented man, became prime minister, could the L-Plan gain some momentum.

The Committee for the Preservation of Agricultural Land (CPAL), the statutory committee with the rule-making power over land designation and consequently over land use, opposed any change of designation from agricultural to urban. The opposition to the development benefitted from the CPAL's position. In addition, one member of the CPAL is always a representative of Israel's Land Management Authority (LMA), which is linked to the Ministry of Agriculture. The LMA was the formal owner of the 200 acres of public land in the "L" area, and could therefore formally block development.

Thus, so far, the controversy involved a variety of powerful organizations, and even the prime minister. Whereas the municipality's position stemmed from a defined need for development and desire for growth, opposition arguments dealt predominantly with societal values and the implications of those values for the nature of urban development, if not for the whole of Israeli society. The translation of these normative positions to decision structures, conflict and action is at the heart of our analysis.

## The Bases of Opposition

A number of arguments (relating to security, agriculture, growth, population dispersal, and urban renewal) were put forward by the oppositionists. It was argued that a country under continuous threat of war should not increase population in its major urban center — which already housed a large part of Israel's population. Possible aircraft attacks were cited. Minister Dayan's recognized military expertise proved to be a valuable resource for the opposition. As former army Chief of Staff, the security argument carried weight, as did his position of leadership in the Ministry of Agriculture. However, Dayan's security arguments against the L-Plan should be assessed against the background of national state issues, namely his ongoing struggle with the Mapai party leadership.[1]

The need to preserve agricultural land was another major argument used against the L-Plan. As noted earlier, the development of agriculture and the preservation of agricultural land has been a traditional and respected norm since pre-state days. In the years following the establishment of the state this principle became a strongly entrenched agrarian interest through such statutory organizations as the CPAL and various settlement movements which had access to decision centers. The agrarian principle was manipulated for specific interests. The agriculturalists' typical arguments were linked to economic-related advantages (e.g., that vegetables could be grown in the L-Plan area before the warm season began in Europe, and could earn much-needed foreign currency).

Those opposing the L-Plan were also concerned about the trend toward urbanization and the growing emphasis on industrial development. They could not halt it, but proposed that urban growth and industrial expansion should take place systematically and deliberately via planning. Symbolism also played its part. It was implied that Israel, where the Jewish people were to find redemption through closeness to the land, was fast urbanizing. Developing the L-Plan area meant that Tel Aviv would soon become contiguous with semi-agricultural towns north of it. To the opposition forces, the crossing of the Yarkon on the west meant growth, change, and relentless, creeping urbanization.

While one can generalize about the political determinants of planning policy, political policy struggles have no prerequisites of consistency. A glaring example of inconsistency is the fact that adjacent to the L-Plan area, to the east, stands Ramat Aviv, a neighborhood in which immigrant housing was built by public authorities on previously cultivated land. Whereas the L-Plan area was, for the most part, sandy and privately owned, the densely populated Ramat Aviv originally stood on public land. Some of the opposing ministries were attempting to change the designation of the L-Plan area from private land to public use, when they had already, in fact, built private housing on public land in the Ramat Aviv area.

The leftist Mapam party opposed growth on ideological and political grounds. They hoped that the Labor mayor of Tel Aviv would not continue to promote the development pattern begun by previous Center Liberal party mayors and would also try to check urban growth. The Mapam Minister of Interior, as noted, proposed a political strategy: belittle the agricultural argument by insisting on a legitimate urban argument — the need for green belts.

Both the security and agricultural arguments were closely linked to the official national policy of population dispersal. The many new immigrant communities that were established along the northern border of the country reflected settlement policies which identified physical presence with security, while promoting agriculture as the main economic base. The population dispersal argument was seized on by the LMA. And in its 1964/65 annual report it demanded that the Government determine the population density of Tel Aviv, including the L-Plan area. The LMA maintained that there was a striking gap between the national policy of population dispersal and actual market-evolved primacy trends, which are also reflected in the city's planning and implementation; in effect, they argued, new facts had been established that were in direct contradiction to the official government policy.[2] The LMA's position illustrates our argument that opposition occurs when major values are called into question. In the present issue, urban growth was challenged by a number of societal norms such as security, agriculture and population dispersal.

Population dispersal policy is an important policy, especially in newly-emerging countries. It is sometimes linked to the specific sectors and interests. In Israel, in the decade following 1948, national population dispersal policy and sectorial interests converged and provided the impetus for the establishment of a great many agricultural settlements. As noted in chapter two, in Israel, population dispersal reflects a developmental concept of settlement and especially a notion of defense (based on a Jewish presence along the borders of Israel). The policy is traceable to the early 1920s, when the policy was conceived as a cornerstone of Jewish settlement policy in Palestine, and later in modern Israel. In spite of this national commitment, the policy fell short of its target — a clear testament of the attracting power of major urban centers. In the contest over the L-Plan, the City of Tel Aviv responded to the population dispersal argument by pointing to the dynamic growth of its own satellite cities, such as Holon and Bat Yam.[3] It was argued that had the policy of population dispersal truly been successful, Tel Aviv would not have stood in its way. This was indeed a compelling argument as it was evident that the population dispersal policy which emerged did not, without government intervention, populate remote areas such as Kiryat Shmona in the north, or Beersheba in the south. Nor did it hinder gravitation to cities such as Ramat Gan, Givatayim, Bat Yam and Holon — all adjacent to Tel Aviv.

The confrontations over the L-Plan offer ample evidence that in a political system such as Israel's, major urban planning policy cannot and is not isolated from the national political arena, its actors, and national norms. Prime Minister Ben-Gurion, chairman of the Committee for the Dispersal of Population, and Dayan, Minister of Agriculture, in arguing against the L-Plan, adhered to considerations not directly related to the defined needs of the leadership of the urban center, but rather to national goals of population dispersal and the reclamation of desolate areas. But more importantly, national actors not only present points of view and assert positions on urban planning, they also have influence on national, authoritative organizations with veto power. Organizations such as the LMA and the CPAL have a direct effect on urban area decisions, and are likely to be guided by the national policy of population dispersal. This is especially the case when powerful actors become involved in a city's planning policy effort.

Analysis of the issue of population dispersal and its role in the politics of urban-planning policy reveals an interdependent system of organization and norms, a situation which is likely to generate conflict and would thus require modes of conflict resolution such as persuasion, influence, use of a power position, compromise, and determination of guiding norms. It is an open conflict arena which, due to interdependence and inter-organizational relations, reaches consensus by politics — either voluntarily, cooperatively, or by imposition.

In resurrecting erstwhile dormant social issues inherent to the long-dominant socialist ruling bodies, opponents of the proposed L-Plan argued that the area should be made into a public park for the benefit of the poor and urban dwellers, rather than a high-rent housing development which could only benefit a wealthy few. A park, of course, would retain the agricultural status of the L-Plan area. It seems likely that this argument was brought forward so that the area could be used for agricultural purposes later — especially since the suggestion was put forth by the strong agricultural lobby, the Agricultural Center (*Hamerkaz Hachaklayi*), which represented the anti-urban development position. The kibbutzim, whose interests were also represented by this lobby, have a rather meager record of accomplishments in absorbing or improving the lot of the poorer segments of Israeli society, although they are certainly ideologically committed to equality. It is doubtful whether in this instance they were inspired by such praiseworthy motives rather than competing for national resources and thus against urban development. Not unlike other organizations, the agricultural sector has not been unknown to demand special advantages and conditions. In the past, for example, it has often obtained water rates and financing at a cheaper rate than that for the urban sector or residents.

It is true, of course, that resources invested in the development of the L-Plan area could conceivably have been made at the expense of urban renewal projects, which up to the 1970s had not been numerous. But such trade-offs are not common and we would be hard pressed to locate empirical evidence for budgets reallocated to slum clearance. Namir, the mayor of Tel Aviv, argued that the L-Plan was not aimed at slum clearance or low income housing, because these were national responsibilities, not local ones. In addition, private investment capital was readily available for the L-Plan, and most of the infrastructure costs would also be covered by private capital.

On both sides of the controversy, organizations dutifully promoted specific norms or interests: on one side stood the Landowners' Association and the municipality; on the other, the ministries, the Inter-Ministerial Committee, the CPAL and the LMA. The conflict was fought not only in the statutory planning organizations, but in governmental agencies, ministries and at the local council level as well. Involvement of powerful organizations and individuals occurs then, when major societal norms — real or perceived interests — are called into question.

## Political Positions and Arenas

Tel Aviv's planning policy of development can be placed in the context of the confrontations over dominance. The organizations that became involved in the politics of the L-Plan planning policy were either mobilized, acted according to dominant norms, or manipulated societal norms for specific political needs.

Mayor Namir, and later Mayor Rabinowitz, assessed the opposition to the L-Plan in political terms. Both sought the support of higher authorities in the government to influence the regular planning organizations and other interested national organizations involved in planning. They solicited the support of the national center-left parties and factions, and a coalition of key Mapai (Labor) figures. To gain support, they also manipulated national norms — from urban growth to the issue of immigrant absorption. They pointed out that Israel's national immigration policy would benefit by urban development because potential new immigrants wish to live in urban areas, not in a remote hinterland. By linking urban growth to the national norm and policy of mass immigration, they argued for the expansion of Tel Aviv, even at the expense of the equally important national norm and policy of population dispersal. Indeed, in the late 1960s, urban development was so sufficiently legitimized that Mayor Rabinowitz launched a development plan for Tel Aviv under the slogan "grow or wither."

The urban survival argument was brought out in the effort to overcome opposition to development; the very survival of Tel Aviv was made a salient issue. It was argued that Jerusalem was emerging as the nation's capital and that attempts were being made to transfer many businesses, newspapers and other institutions there. The need to maintain Tel Aviv as the metropolitan center of the country was repeatedly raised by both planners and politicians who advanced the L-Plan. The alternative, so the city leadership argued, was to limit immigration — an unthinkable policy for Israel, notwithstanding urban congestion and problems.

The struggle over the L-Plan demonstrates that in a political system such as Israel's, urban (planning) policy can neither be isolated from national politics, nor can actors be immune to the effect of national norms. National actors not only assert positions on urban area planning policy, but also wield influence on powerful organizations which often have direct authority and veto power over urban area decisions. In the conflict over the L-Plan area, the CPAL and the LMA were guided by and committed to those actors who advocated the national policy of population dispersal.

## Strategies and Outcomes

Analysis of the strategies used by national actors, and the process of overcoming opposition, are central to the understanding of the politics of planning policy. The strategies that actors adopt are related to the structures that actors belong to and policies they value. They are likely to activate a number of resources and use them judiciously. Resources are likely to include appeal and exclusion, access to decision centers, and alliance-building.

In the early 1950s the L-Plan called for low-density building and community centers, including a park. The first to appeal these planning conceptions was the Landowners Association (AL), which used its resources in order to pressure the planning organizations. It appealed a number of times to the courts in an effort to secure a ruling favoring development, to increase the population density of the city plan. By doing this they added value to the large tracts of land and specific parcels they owned. Their legal action was intended to make the RPBC and CPAL take some action. The landowners' concern over development was also related to their specific interests regarding the statutory 40 percent appropriation of the land for public use. The appropriation raised the question of how the remaining land would be divided among them. The pressure from organized groups led the City of Tel Aviv to respond willingly by establishing a special municipal development organization to handle the L-Plan area.

The Ministry of Interior, aided by the CPAL, activated their political resource of exclusion by removing the plan from the agenda. The ministry declared that the L-Plan could not be considered so long as the land was classified as agricultural. They attempted to make it a "non-issue" and proceeded via the RPBC to cancel all previous plans for the L-Plan area. Their move was supported by the Ministry of Agriculture, which prepared an alternative plan to develop up to 80 percent of the area for agricultural purposes. Threat of appeal to the Supreme Court from the Landowners Association led the Ministry of Interior to declare that their negation of old plans referred only to public land and not to private rights in the area. This removed the possibility of possible demands for compensation to private land owners. The planned negation of plans later proved unnecessary because a coalition between the Ministry of Interior, the Ministry of Agriculture and the CPAL was sufficient in keeping the L-Plan a non-issue by retaining its agricultural status and thus making all plans irrelevant.

The negation and blocking of municipal plans was undertaken by national organizations, which thereby defined the conflict arena. The city was forced to approach national decision-making organizations in order to remove nationally-set obstacles. In late 1959 the city of Tel Aviv initiated a confrontation by utilizing the mayor's political links to a national decision center. Namir's strong position within the Tel Aviv branch of the Labor party made it possible for him to have access and to appeal to the prime minister. Namir asked him to convene the cabinet-level Economic Affairs Committee (chaired by the powerful Minister Eshkol, a close associate of the mayor), in order to outline possible uses for the L-Plan area. Faced with this action, the Ministers of Interior and Agriculture appealed before the full cabinet meeting and succeeded in delaying any decision. They further succeeded in preempting any action by the city, being mindful of an important feature of the Israeli political-administrative culture, namely that that which is initiated and implemented, sometimes even illegally, stands a good chance of being continued. Thus, it was important for opponents of the L-Plan to establish at cabinet level that no steps would be taken by any authority which would create physical facts that might influence a future governmental decision. This would block any action-oriented types of implementation by the city. This action can be compared to the government's stance over Jerusalem, where the action-oriented planning by the Ministry of Housing was supported by the government and was a major obstacle to the city's evolution of its own planning policy (see chapter 5).

## Alliance-Building

Leadership is a crucial resource in determining planning policy, but where conflict is involved, it is essential. Implementation is often hampered in the absence of leadership. Following the

175

October 1959 elections, Namir, the proponent of urban development, became mayor of Tel Aviv. Bar-Yehuda, the Mapam party
Minister of Interior who opposed urban growth, did not return to
the government. The changed political scene gave Mayor
Namir's active interest in development of the L-Plan area a new
momentum, and new chances for achieving desired outcomes.

Namir immediately proceeded to draw up a plan for the area.
His strategy was to form alliances with key figures in the government who were members of his political faction (Mapai). The
alliance with the Minister of Finance (Eshkol) bore fruit and
Namir's position within the city stood to gain. In 1961, Eshkol
brought before the government and the CPAL a proposal to redes-
ignate the L-Plan area as urban land and to annul the prohibition
on building in the area. Eshkol assisted his political allies in Tel
Aviv by creating a national issue out of an urban question. The
help he gave the city was based on political alliances; the arguments before the government had to be national. As the key economic figure in the government, Eshkol referred to the country's
need for economic development. His proposal to change the designated land was justified by indicating that foreign investment
capital was readily available to develop the area, and foreign capital and currency was what the country was short of.

Economic viability was presented as an important national
issue. Eshkol's intervention made salient the convergence of local and national interests and thus helped to overcome the national concerns over population dispersal, as well as the dominant
rural interests. Eshkol mobilized other agencies, such as the National Investment Authority, which was under his jurisdiction as
Minister of Finance. He stressed that this was an opportunity for
utilizing foreign funds to purchase and build on public land — a
deliberate ploy in order to prevent the release of private land from
agricultural status and thus avoid the escalation of land values
through speculation. *Haaretz*, which usually favors business,
warned that this proposal would result in expansion of housing,
construction and development in the entire area north of Tel
Aviv.[4] Even though the open space issue was popular, the government accepted Eshkol's plea for construction on public land. Noting the government's approval, the Regional Planning and
Building Commission agreed, in principle, not to oppose the
change in the agricultural status of the area, should the request
come before the CPAL, and to accept the initial outline plan which
the City of Tel Aviv had prepared.

Encouraged by this initial success, the municipality returned to its earlier attempt to promote the L-Plan by means of a special municipal organization. In 1962, the municipality — this time with government financial support — established a semi-public corporation for the development of the L-Plan area.[5] The social, economic and political ramifications of the issue, and the political involvement of a variety of actors, led the city to define the corporation's role narrowly, within the limits of approved plans only. It recognized and encouraged the right of private and public organizations to have access to a decision-making role in the plan. The development corporation was to negotiate with various landowners and foreign investors. The municipality then moved from alliance-building politics to increasing its own economic stake by the acquisition of physical resources. The city owned some 180 acres in the L-Plan area, and pressured the government to sell it 200 acres of public land in the area. The development corporation was expanded and the scope of its negotiations increased to include public financial institutions. As rewards seemed imminent, more private firms joined in. But opponents of the plan, via national organizations and personalities with statutory and political power, again opposed its implementation.

In January 1963, the Inter-Ministerial Committee on Population Dispersal announced that it opposed the development of the L-Plan area. Dayan, the Minister of Agriculture, used his power through the governmental managerial structure. He instructed the LMA, which was under his ministry's jurisdiction, not to sell public land to the City of Tel Aviv. The Inter-Ministerial Committee argued against urban primacy and in favor of the development of the more remote cities, such as Ashdod or Ashkelon. The Ministry of Housing, which normally builds in the more remote areas, supported the population dispersal position and was against private and city initiatives of development such as the L-Plan. In addition, the ministry raised an argument that had been previously used by the Ministry of Interior, namely that no outline plan had yet been completed for the city and therefore the L-Plan should first be integrated with a comprehensive plan. These developments, reflecting organizational positions which, in turn, sided with the contention that additional population in the L-Plan area was a security risk, were a major setback to the L-Plan and its proponents.

The ability of organizations in a centrist system such as Israel's to block a policy should be emphasized, since this ability has implications concerning planning policy and policy in general. Specifically we can identify: (1) relative independence of each organization in the governmental structure and the institutionalization of these organizations' domains; (2) the nature of a centrist political system which brings about convergence of its parts via conflict resolution and the process of consensus making (the immediate implication is that each of the parts needs to be taken into account, or to be overcome either by a stronger force or by a coalition); (3) upon analyzing the state's government structure, one finds that more divergent forces exist than one is usually led to believe. In the discussion below we analyze how opposition is overcome through the creation of strong coalitions.

## Policy Outcomes in a Local-National System

The veto position on the L-Plan of the Inter-Ministerial Committee on Population Dispersal was most ominous to the city and its leadership, because it represented a national policy which enjoyed a high consensus. Thus, Mayor Namir faced a national political arena involved in a local policy. The mayor reactivated his faction in the national party (i.e., the Mapai party ministers), in order to secure support for the L-Plan and to overcome Dayan, who belonged to an opposition faction in the party. He attacked the issue on a political and urban basis. He prudently involved his party. Namir believed that failure to overcome opposition would cost the Labor party the mayoralty of Tel Aviv.[6] He noted that surrounding cities offered cheaper housing than Tel Aviv, and that the influx of people to these areas resulted in a diminished tax base, and therefore burdened Tel Aviv's ability to provide services.

The Mayor's party affiliates were sympathetic, but they could offer no immediate solutions. Prime Minister Ben-Gurion, who could not be overruled, insisted on the issue of population dispersal. The Labor party in the early 1960s was torn by many conflicts. An urban development was not likely to be the issue over which dissidents wanted to confront Ben-Gurion. As to the policy of population dispersal, the government, while arguing against population concentration in Tel Aviv, was itself building high density housing in neighboring cities as well as in neighborhoods of Tel Aviv. Unfortunately for Tel Aviv, the L-Plan became a "last stand" type of issue for those opposed to a change toward more urbanism. These confrontations were exacerbated by the struggle within the Labor party.

The identification of an actor's motivations helps to explain his political involvement, as do his stakes in a policy.[7] The struggle within the Labor party motivated many to become involved. This struggle threatened the planning process. Yet the same actors had also to eventually enact an appropriate planning policy. It is likely that when a planning issue involves such intense political involvement (because of factors irrelevant to the original plan), it takes on a momentum of its own and distorts the planning issue. Dayan, for example, needed issues to confront the Labor party's Mapai faction. He had a clear stake in generating conflict, and the resources to do it. As an alternative to the L-Plan he suggested the rebuilding of the ancient city of Modi'in near the pre-1967 border with Jordan. This suggestion was both a powerful resource and ploy in Dayan's political struggle against the L-Plan. In addition to paying homage to the security argument, the choice of Modi'in would contribute to the much-desired Jewish presence in an area of importance to the state. Moreover, the site of Modi'in had religious and historical significance to Israelis, as the location of a (victorious) Maccabean battle. Planning in Tel Aviv had become a part of the struggle within the Labor party and a victim of it.

The notion that the identification of actors, their motivations and interactions, can explain involvement and policy conflict is also relevant when resolutions to the conflict begin to appear. In part, this occurred due to changes in the government. In 1963, Ben-Gurion resigned as prime minister; Eshkol (the national Labor party ally of the mayor of Tel Aviv) became the prime minister. To Eshkol, the L-Plan issue meant support for a key member of his political group — Namir. At this juncture, each of the opponents of the L-Plan had to decide whether an urban development issue was what they wanted to confront the new prime minister with. New policy guidelines were set by Prime Minister Eshkol and Minister of the Treasury Sapir, the head of the LMA Weitz, the Deputy Mayor of Tel Aviv Rabinowitz, and by Namir and Dayan. The guidelines were a breakthrough toward a resolution of the conflict. It was decided that the prohibition on the start of development of the L-Plan area should be modified. The wide publicity over the issue was a key factor. To pacify Dayan, it was decided to approve Namir's plans on non-government land only; the fate of the public land was left open to negotiation. The earlier decision — taken by the Ministry of Housing — prohibiting development on the grounds of population dispersal was thus negated.

As a feature of the policy-making process in Israel, these new decisions also reflected modes of conflict resolution which created a more positive setting, wherein old confrontations were now defined as part of an ongoing and legitimate debate. It was not announced — neither by the city nor by the government — that a new policy was being undertaken. Nevertheless the Minister of Interior, A. Shapira, remained a strong opponent to the L-Plan. In the federated structure of government, which allots areas of responsibility to coalition partners, he had to defend his domain vis-a-vis the Labor leaders. His view of the planning of the L-Plan area reflected that of his planning department, namely that the area should become part of a green belt around Tel Aviv that would protect further planned development. The minister and his staff adhered to the veto decision of the Inter-Ministerial Committee on Population Dispersal, which prohibited development in the L-Plan area. He argued that procedurally this was a binding governmental decision, as was the declaration of the area as agricultural land. He maintained that a change in designation required redesignation and approval procedures. In order to maintain a political role Shapira attempted to reemphasize procedure, even though the issue had become completely politicized.

The Minister of Interior's position had to be taken seriously — not because Israeli policy-making processes and actors are necessarily always sensitive to precedent and procedure — but rather because the power position of the minister would enable him to trigger a major political confrontation within the coalition government. The Minister of Interior had to protect his (and his planning department's) place and function in urban planning. Thus, city leaders once again had to evolve new strategies. But this time, with the support of key government members, it would be easier.

As Shapira raised his opposition, three parallel events took place. First, Deputy Mayor Rabinowitz signed an agreement with the LMA, transferring the public land of the L-Plan area to the Municipal Development Corporation. Second, the Ministry of Agriculture began work on Dayan's plan for the new city of Modi'in. Third, Rabinowitz appealed to the Inter-Ministerial Committee on Population Dispersal, requesting that building be allowed in the L-Plan area; this amounted to a request for cancellation of the standing veto prohibiting development. This formal move to overcome the Minister of Interior's opposition was successful, for the composition of the committee had now changed. Previously, the committee had been headed by Ben-Gurion; now when Rabinowitz appealed, it was chaired by the Mayor of Tel Aviv's political ally, Prime Minister Eshkol. Nevertheless, the Minister of Interior was given his due — only partial development was granted. At the same time the Minister of Agriculture was given a role in the planning of Modi'in. In late December 1963, 500 acres in the L-Plan area were released for construction as urban land. Soon after, a plan was drawn up by the City of Tel Aviv and approved by the local and regional planning commissions. Concurrently, the plan for Modi'in received additional momentum.

We have shown that in Israel, ministries and other organizations enjoy a high degree of independent decision-making and action as a result of the offices themselves being the spoils of the political confrontation between factions and parties. This structure generates different coalitions at different times. In the L-Plan case, a winning coalition emerged which overcame the opposition of the Ministries of Interior and Agriculture, as well as the agricultural veto.

The Municipal Development Corporation began negotiating with landowners regarding compensation claims, in the event that they might be affected by confiscation. Contractors, businesses and banks joined in the development efforts. It appeared that many, including former opponents, now had a new stake in securing a share in the development of the L-Plan area. One such organization was the Contractors Association. By the end of 1964, the transfer of LMA-controlled public lands to the city was agreed upon and signed; at the same time the city allocated funds for the development of infrastructure. Namir, the mayor, who had been able to increase the city's economic base, could now claim that he had fulfilled his election campaign promise to develop the L-Plan area.

Thus far we have seen how the overcoming of opposition requires skills in alliance-building, exchanging resources, and understanding and identifying the scope of the interorganizational relationships between those institutions which form part of the decision structure and involvement in planning politics. The next step is to ask why individuals or organizations become involved in planning conflict, and what triggers their involvement.

## Local Politics and Policy Involvement

The decisions concerning the L-Plan were affected by normative societal factors, and interests represented by ministries, agencies, and organized groups. There was little direct public involvement. During the 1960s (and indeed, even to this day), the opportunities for the Israeli public to take a stand and become directly involved in a planning issue are limited, especially when elites begin to bargain. However, planning policies that are made salient by press coverage and conflict between elites have a stimulating effect on the local scene and on organizations and individuals. In the present case the role of the Contractors Association and the small landowners is especially important. The interests of the Contractors Association were represented via the Tel Aviv City Council; the association was thus able to exert significant pressure and influence on municipal and planning decisions.

In the rest of the chapter we analyze the contest over the L-Plan on the local level. This analysis is undertaken in order to further explicate what triggers involvement in planning conflict, the intensity and types of local opposition in local planning policy, and the enactment and implementation process. These factors are important to an understanding of the politics of planning.

The L-Plan triggered the political involvement of not only powerful national organizations but also a range of local ones. The Tel Aviv Municipal Council in particular became deeply involved with the L-Plan. As a rule, the structure of local planning modifies the opposition of local planning organizations, since the members of the local planning bodies are also members of the local council. Only minor opposition to a dominant mayor is likely, because the council usually represents a disciplined coalition structure. A strong mayor is certain to keep a tight rein over his coalition. Persistent resistance by a coalition partner or even by an opposition party can be overcome by distributing personal and public rewards. Generally, there is likely to be a lower intensity of opposition to a planning policy in the local arena, in contrast to the high intensity confrontations involving normative features when ministries, the CPAL or the Inter-Ministerial Committee on Population Dispersal is involved. In the L-Plan controversy, the local demand groups operated through the local council.

The political leadership of Tel Aviv wanted the various agreements with allies in national organizations to become the basis for technical planning. It wanted to avoid new opposition, which might arise unexpectedly from local sources, and which would increase the number of stakeholders in the L-Plan area project. At the same time, however, the mayor of Tel Aviv was inclined to accommodate the major demand organizations — including pressure groups such as the Contractors Association and the Landowners Associations. Opposition groups found the coalition structure of the Tel Aviv Council a convenient vehicle through which to make their demands a public issue. Such groups cannot threaten coalition discipline, but they can arouse public attention and provoke others who have decision-making powers to effectively oppose plans. This structure explains why opposition parties at the local level are often accommodated.

## The Contractors Association

The membership of the Municipal Development Corporation, established to manage the development of the L-Plan, was a source of conflict. The issue involved demands for a share in future decision making and the distribution of economic benefits. Center-right party members of the local coalition demanded that the Contractors Association be included in the corporation. The Labor-dominated Tel Aviv Council rejected the demand, arguing that the contractors had a direct economic interest in construction, and therefore should not be included. A leftist Mapam representative demanded that the council forbid any member of the corporation from undertaking commercial construction in the L-Plan area. Each political group assumed a position consistent with an ideological policy, or on behalf of a constituency. Conflict over substantive planning policy is exacerbated as a result of interests represented among contestants, irrespective of the planning issue. When the Labor forces overruled the center and right-wing party members, the latter encouraged the Contractors Association to appeal to the Supreme Court for a fair share of the project. Faced by this suit, the local council decided that the Municipal Development Corporation should become public. The Contractors Association immediately joined in the commercial venture. There was a full exchange of resources; the contractors rescinded their threat of appeal to the Supreme Court, and in turn they were allowed to buy land and to participate in the building of the L-Plan area. The three major commercial banks, the government mortgage bank, a public land company, and a public investment company were registered with the proposed corporation. By July 1966, the LMA had transferred about 350 acres of which 37 percent was zoned as residential, 22 percent as commercial and seashore, and 41 percent for tourism. The cost was assessed accordingly.[8] The major local parties agreed to propose that municipal construction projects would not require public bidding.[9]

The contractors' economic stakes were clear, and they fought for a share in a profitable economic enterprise. Following initial approval of the plan, prices of land soared and the entire L-Plan area became a place of lucrative development. Accommodation of pressure groups is not idiosyncratic in Israel's corporatist structure. Opposition is usually overcome by either cooptation or by sharing the enterprise involved or the rewards. In addition the contractors had great nuisance value because they could have blocked or delayed implementation. They could have won a temporary injunction in their appeal to the Supreme Court, basing their case on the fact that the transfer of land from the LMA to the municipal corporation was illegal.[10] Unlike the national figures who advanced arguments against the entire plan, the Contractors Association (and their allies on the council) were more concrete: they simply wanted a share in the development. Gaining a share is legitimized in Israel's political culture. Their position indicates that generation of conflict and a capacity for obstruction enhances accommodation.

## Ministerial Positions

Conflict over the planning policy of the L-Plan did not end with accommodations made to the Contractors Association; other interests continued to try and penetrate the local decision-making arena in order to assure their stakes. The sale agreement between the LMA and the City of Tel Aviv generated many requests for land allotment from the municipality. The Histadrut Labor Federation requested land for housing projects for the elderly; the electric company wanted land in order to expand their power complex, which already stood in the L-Plan area; and the municipal bus company requested space for terminal grounds.

Technical preparation of the L-Plan was entrusted to the LPBC. Actual detailed planning began in mid-1964, and concurrently the city provided funds for infrastructure. But even as planning and implementation was being carried out and publicized, attempts to limit the city's right to plan were made. Once again, these attempts were motivated by political considerations.

Dayan, who was no longer Minister of Agriculture, seized on the national-local land-sale agreement in order to again oppose development of the L-Plan area. In his resurgent opposition he now used the Knesset. He submitted a formal request to the new Minister of Agriculture for information concerning the particulars of the sale of public land to the Municipal Development Corporation. In April 1965, a reply was given; it revealed few unknown details relating to the division of the L-Plan area into public, private and institutional designations. In July 1965, Ben-Gurion, who was at that time at the peak of his struggle with the Mapai (Labor) leadership, argued against implementing the L-Plan on the basis of the security and population dispersal arguments. This time, however, the momentum of the plan was not stopped, as it had been when he was head of the Inter-Ministerial Committee on Population Dispersal and could assume a powerful veto role in planning. These last minute attempts to obstruct were not successful, because neither Dayan nor Ben-Gurion any longer controlled an organization involved in planning, such as the LMA. Neither did government agencies at this stage undertake a parallel planning or action-oriented planning policy, as was the case in the planning of Jerusalem. The city remained dominant in the actual planning. Indeed, the city and the Development Corporation proceeded with detailed planning in an area of about 70 acres designated for apartment buildings.

The politics involving the RPBC was the last potential threat to city policy. The member cities on the RPBC were expected to support the L-Plan; such a development would be an important precedent for any city which wanted to control its planning policy and its economic structure by the expansion of its tax base. The ministerial representatives were no longer free to influence decisions, given that the coalition government's support was assured by Prime Minister Eshkol, who guaranteed the ministers' agreement at the ministerial level and of course influenced their representatives on the RPBC. Dayan and Ben-Gurion held no governmental positions and were in an all-out political struggle with Eshkol, which led to their secession from the Labor party in 1965.

Specific plans for the entire L-Plan area were announced in the city's budget debate of 1966-67, and actual construction followed. The earlier tactic of planning for low-density housing, used as a means of securing approval, was abandoned and the city decided to double the density allotted to the earlier plans. Also, some of the areas designated for public use were reduced, as were the number of public service designations. For example, plans for only 15 instead of 19 public schools were included. Final agreement over the transfer of land from the LMA was publicly signed. Actual approval of the L-Plan by the RPBC followed.[11]

The plan called for the construction of private and public housing. After appropriation of the obligatory 40 percent for public purposes, a density of 10 units per quarter acre was determined. Over the 60 days in which the plan was deposited for public review with the RPBC much opposition was registered, notably from the Ministry of Interior, its Planning Department, and from private landowners. At this point the ministry attempted to reassert its right to determine specific procedural-technical planning matters, including density. But it was too late; a major political contest had been resolved. Not only were most of the objections presented to the RPBC rejected, but in August 1968 the plans were even extended northward of the area originally approved. In 1969, Sapir, the powerful Minister of Finance and close political ally of the Tel Aviv political machine, participated in the opening of the first housing project in the L-Plan area.

From the political analysis perspective, we can note an incremental development in the planning politics of the L-Plan. Many aspects of it were approved gradually, at different intervals; decisions were slow but well-designed and binding, and were used as a foundation by the initiator — the Tel Aviv City Council — to push forward its development policy.

## The Private Landowners

The opposition of the private landowners came to the fore when actual implementation of the development began. Their opposition was related to the Municipal Development Corporation's plans to appropriate land in the early stages of development, when the cost of land was still relatively low. The corporation proceeded to commission a formal, public assessment of the value of the land in order to establish a basis on which to negotiate with the landowners; with its own vested interests in the development of the LPA, it attempted to secure low cost land rights from private owners — an action heavily criticized in the press. The major political lesson for interest groups was that in order to apply pressure, they had to organize well. The private landowners were not organized so as to confront what appeared to be speculation on public lands. As planning and implementation progressed, they eventually succeeded in establishing an organized front and formed an association to handle their claims. The new association, given the experience of other organized groups, had a better chance to deal with the awesome forces that were involved in the development of the area. And the private landowners had many issues to deal with. For example, some of the public utilities, including a municipal beach, were planned on private land; their owners were not immediately compensated, while at the same time the owners were obligated to pay taxes on this land to the city and, up to the 1970s, to the government.

The private landowners were the least effective in the L-Plan area controversy. The political lesson of organization for defense of interests was learned too late. In the end they applied for compromises and settlement within the courts or with the municipality. They were too slow in utilizing a potential and useful alliance with the Ministry of Interior, which suggested court action to compel the city to construct only public institutions on public land. The major tactic used against the individual landowners by the city was the municipality's refusal to parcel or detail plans of plots belonging to the private landowners, thus preventing construction. The municipality's planning conception was related to the tactic which forced early development on public land, thus mandating many private lots to public use and services. The pressure on private landowners led to a sale of some of the privately owned land to the city, which allocated compensation, either at relatively low rates or by the granting of plots in alternative sites.

The municipality proposed its compensation on the basis of ownership minus the 40 percent to which it is entitled without compensation.[12] Under such an arrangement the small landowners were severely penalized. Occasionally, in order to avoid court litigation, the municipal corporation agreed on marked price compensation based on projected potential building rights. Development and construction contracts, in turn, were awarded to large public and private companies. It appears that individuals who are not represented by a formal lobbying organization are less likely to be effective in dealings with municipal public agencies. Nevertheless, individuals do have recourse to the courts.

Most of the objections that were raised over the 60 days within which the plan was on public display in the RPBC were overruled by the local and central coalition consensus. During the political confrontation over the L-Plan, the city promised opponents to high density plans large plots and a low number of dwelling units per lot. The actual density averaged 13 units to a quarter of an acre, double the number of units in the earlier plans. Once the conflict over the agriculture designation, open space, population dispersal, security, and ruralism vs. urban growth was eliminated, the L-Plan went urban all the way. In the implementation stage, familiar budgetary problems emerged to plague the city. Efforts were made to save infrastructure costs while increasing the potential tax base of the area. These deviations were made possible by political interactions of the local government and its allies on the RPBC.

The confrontation over the L-Plan area planning policy had features of confrontation between elites: power and influence were key factors. Thus the question of whether the L-Plan area was well-planned and designed is somewhat secondary to the planning policy decision process. The unheeded warnings voiced by many opponents of the L-Plan — quality of urban life factors, such as building density, population concentration, congestion, environmental factors and excessive urbanism — are well on their way to becoming realities. Development continues onward north of the area. The new struggle over the nature of future development is underway, but is not loaded with the normative features of the original politics over the L-Plan. Individuals who own land in the northern part of the area learned the value of organizing in order to be effective. It is fought out in the courts, and in the LPBC and RPBC.

The discussion of the contests over the planning policy in the L-Plan underscores a number of characteristics of the politics of planning and development in Israel. Firstly, systemic, structural and normative features bear directly on urban development planning. Because values, norms and interests are involved in planning development, action on the part of statutory planning organizations takes place only after the various organizations involved in planning (which represent these norms) are accommodated or their opposition overcome. Secondly, several national institutions and their political alliances play a direct role in urban planning policy. Thirdly, it appears that actual, detailed land-use planning becomes relevant only after principles of policy are worked out politically by local and national organizations and institutions. Deviations from prior positions are possible, especially in the light of changing coalitions and conditions. In the case of the L-Plan, such changes enabled the city to overcome opposition based on the powerful normative position regarding population dispersal. The preservation of agricultural land was also used as a resource in the confrontation over the plan, and for a time this blocked development. Israeli planning policy and process is influenced by these factors (for example, through the input of the CPAL in handling planning decisions) in major planning policy confrontations, and also in regular planning processes.

# Notes — Chapter 6

1. Yanai N. *Cleavage at the Top.* Tel Aviv: Levin-Epstein, 1969 (Hebrew); and *Political Crisis in Israel During the Ben-Gurion Period.* Jerusalem: Keter, 1982 (Hebrew).
2. Land Management Authority. *Annual Report.* Jerusalem, 1965/6, pp. 14-19; State Controller. "Land Management Authority," *Annual Report.* No. 37. Jerusalem, 1987, pp. 575-587.
3. Interview with Mayor Y. Rabinowitz.
4. *Haaretz* (21 September 1961).
5. *Minutes*, LPBC, for 1961-1962 and State Controller (1987), No. 37.
6. Conveyed by Mayor Y. Rabinowitz.
7. Saunders, P. (1979) *Urban Politics.* London: Hutchison, 1979; Blowers, A. *The Limits of Power: The Politics of Local Planning Policy.* Oxford: Pergamon, 1980.
8. State Controller (1987), No. 37.
9. The decision could be the basis for an appeal to the Supreme Court since there is a requirement for public bidding of public land.
10. *Ibid.*
11. *Minutes*, RPBC (8 February 1967).
12. *Planning and Building Law.* Jerusalem: Ministry of Interior, 1985.

# ABOUT THE AUTHOR

Efraim Torgovnik teaches at the Department of Political Science, Tel Aviv University. He is the author of *Determinants in Managerial Selection* and articles on "Central Aid and Local Policy," "Effectiveness Assessment in Public Service Systems" (with E. Preisler), and "Local Policy Determinants in a Centrist System." He is past president of the Israel Political Science Association and member of the Council of the International Political Science Association.

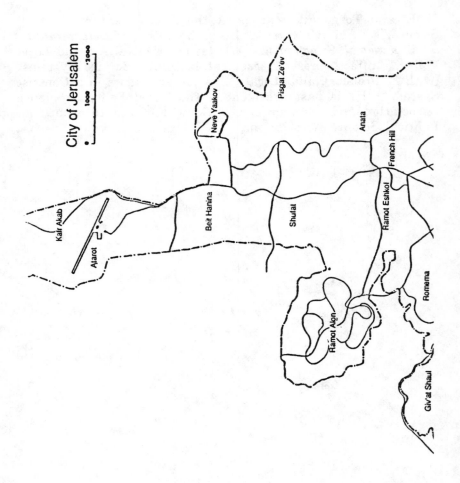

City of Jerusalem

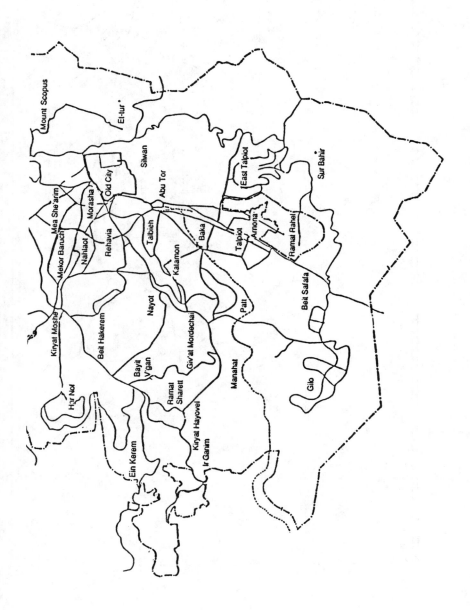

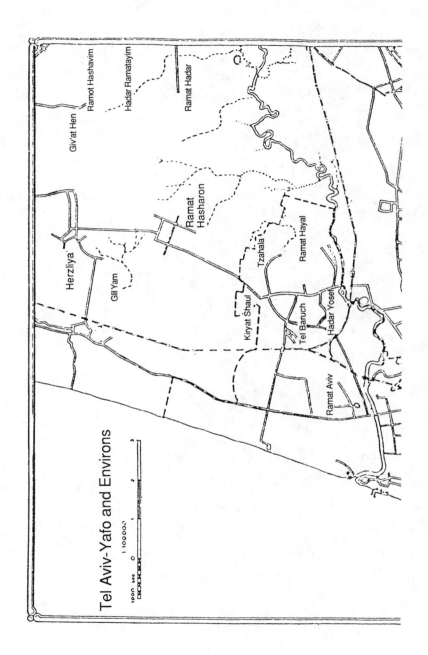

Tel Aviv-Yafo and Environs

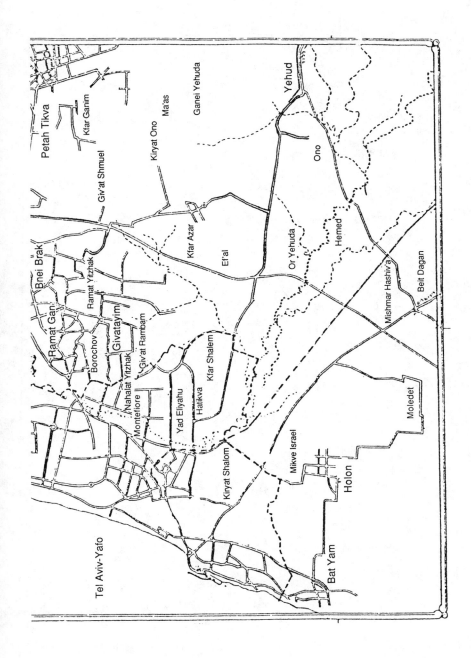